STUDIES IN HIGHER EDUCATION IN

RESEARCH ON HIGHER EDUCATION IN SWEDEN

An Analysis and an Evaluation

Guy Neave
Sally Jenkinson

ALMQVIST & WIKSELL INTERNATIONAL STOCKHOLM

This book is a report to the Advisory Groups of the Research on
Higher Education Program sponsored by the Swedish National
Board of Universities and Colleges (NBUC)

©The Research on Higher Education Program, NBUC
Graphic design and production by PAN EIDOS, Lund
Typesetting by UN-sats, Lund
Almqvist & Wiksell International, Stockholm, 1983
ISBN 91-22-00624-9
ISSN 0280-2988

Contents

Preface

The writing of reports is never a solitary vice and this one is no exception. The origins of this report are to be found in the initiative taken by the advisory groups of the Research into Higher Education Programme of the National Board of Universities and Colleges.In 1981/2, they decided that it would be useful to have an outside evaluation of this programme. It is unlikely, however, that this mission would have fallen to these authors had it not been for the intervention of Professor Kjell Härnqvist of the University of Göteborg and who is now its Rector. He knew of our likely interest in undertaking such a review and offered a working base at his University. Leave of absence was needed for both of us. Dr Ladislav Cerych, Director of the European Institute of Education and Social Policy of the European Cultural Foundation at the University of Paris IX Dauphine, arranged a secondment from that Institute during the period from October 1982 to February 1983. Dr. D. MacDowall, Director of the Polytechnic of North London opened the way for a similar arrangement.

Four months is all too short a period in which to gather the data for an overview of a national research programme and more particularly one which comprises scholars in many disciplines, especially if the language is other than one's own. Sweden embraces a policy of routinely translating research findings into English as an international vehicle of dissemination. The Programme for Research into Higher Education translates both its findings and also its project outlines into English. Without this practice, we could not have undertaken this review. Yet, the longer we stayed, the more aware we became of the need to probe more deeply into Swedish history and culture and thereby the Swedish language as a means of doing justice to the evaluation. Even so, there was and remains more data available in English translation than we could assimilate.

The methods of obtaining and analysing the information we needed, were many. Initially, twenty four formal interviews were arranged with personalities involved in the Programme of Research into Higher Education. Twelve were leading practitioners in Swedish higher education, many of whom had also served on the advisory group of practitioners on the Programme. Twelwe were researchers active in the Programme as project leaders or in other capacities. Conducting these interviews involved much travel within Sweden. Göteborg, Stockholm, Lund, Umeå, Uppsala and Malmö were visited by car, train or plane. It hardly needs saying that informal discussions during and after seminars with the recording machine switched off, were no less instructive than the formal fact-gathering with the machine switched on. This led us to seek out additional information by consulting sources not on our initial agenda and to ask questions that we had not previously thought necessary to pose. Informal – even chance – meetings with various members of the academic and political community added to our knowledge about Sweden and to our capacity for assessing it.

Two working bases rather than one – the first in the Department of Educational Research at the University of Göteborg and the second in the Department of Political Science at the University of Stockholm – kept us reminded that the academic community is made up of individual eccentricity and autonomous disciplines about which generalisations are hazardous. Two evaluators – rather then one – with experience of teaching and research in several disciplines – History, Education, Political Theory and Social Statistics as they operate in several European countries, probably helped in formulating the right questions and in maintaining a scepticism about the validity of conclusions.

The number of people who have helped us to understand the finer points about Swedish higher education, its history, its administration and its financing of research, is vast. To those who contributed to our working arrangements, we must give particular mention and thanks. They include Rector Kjell Härnqvist, Dr Lennart Levin and Dr. Eskil Björklund and all those colleagues who assisted us in the Department of Educational Research at the University of Göteborg and the Department of Political Science at the University of Stockholm and especially Professor Ference Marton, Professor Roger Säljö, Dr. Lennart Svensson and Dr. Lars-Owe Dahlgren at the former and Professor Olof Ruin, Dr. Rune Premfors and Dr. Bjorn Wittrock at the latter, Department.

Many dozens of people interrupted their schedules to reply to our questions. We would like to thank them all and in particular Chancellor Carl-Gustaf Andrén and his predecessor in that office, Mr. Hans Löwbeer, also Professor Hans Landberg, Mr. Lennart Larsson of the TCO and Mr. Erland Ringborg whom we saw in Stockholm. So too, we extend our particular thanks to Dr. Inga Elgqvist-Saltzman and Dr. Jan-Erik Lane of the University of Umeå in the North of Sweden.

Finally, in a work so quickly produced, omissions, errors and infelicities there must be and we take full responsibility for them. Nevertheless, we believe that our overall conclusions about the Swedish Research into

Higher Education Programme are well supported by the evidence we have obtained. In particular, our own conclusions are that by international comparison, the Programme has developed remarkably quickly; that it draws on an encouragingly wide variety of academic disciplines; and that the relationship between government and scholars is finely tuned.

Two appendices are included, the first is a select list of publications arising from the Programme of Research into higher education between 1973 and 1983. The second is a select list of on-going projects currently conducted within the framework of the Programme.

June 1983
G Neave
S Jenkinson

1 Higher education research: research: A short sketch of a broad field

It is a good thing to know something of the customs and manners of various people in order to judge of our own more objectively and so not think everything that is contrary to our own ways is ridiculous and irrational, as those who have seen nothing are in the habit of doing. But when one spends too much time travelling, one becomes eventually a stranger to one's own country: and when one is too interested in what went on in past centuries, one usually remains extremely ignorant of what is happening in this century.

– **René Descartes**, *Discours de la Méthode*, 1637.

Introduction

In Western Europe, the emergence of higher education as a systematic, self-standing area of enquiry, backed by large-scale funding is a comparatively recent development. There has, of course, been a long tradition of scholarly writing undertaken by individuals – historians in the main – dealing with the rise and fall of particular establishments. Yet this individual scholarship has remained, to a considerable extent, peripheral – where not antagonistic – to those more recent developments that have contributed to the rise of higher education as a field of study.[1]

The rise of higher education research

The rise of higher education as a separate subject of scholarly investigation in recent times is the result of two developments. The first involved the penetration into higher education of those disciplines which, during the early Sixties, had already coalesced around the three inter-related issues of secondary education reform, manpower planning and economic growth. The second – and main driving force behind this realignment in the component disciplines in the field of the educational sciences in general, was the need facing governments in Western industrialised countries to seek alternative institutional arrangements. They involved new funding patterns and extended facilities to meet the demographic wave and the additional demand for higher education as both rolled towards the groves of academe. In Sweden, those disciplines which had been instrumental in paving the way for reforming secondary education – political economy, economics and psychology – turned towards higher education as government attention began to focus on that sector of the education system.

Just as in secondary education, these two developments brought about a fundamental change to a domain hitherto dominated by the intellectual requirements of teacher training. So too did they operate a similar transformation in the study of higher education.

An examination of the type of discipline contributing to the academic study of higher education in Sweden during the 1950's suggests that the disciplines well to the fore were psychology, social statistics and economic forecasting. They corresponded to the particular perspective that dominated the debate in Swedish higher education in the 1950's – namely the identification of "reserves of ability" and, no less important, the need to harness the university more closely to the requirements of the national economy. To these were added later, sociology – as a response to the question how far higher education itself might act as an instrument for the eradication of social inequality in access to the higher form of knowledge.

Some ten years ago, towards the start of the Seventies – though obviously the chronology will vary from country to country – the study of higher education saw a further disciplinary influx. It brought in administrative studies, locational science, political science, organisation theory and government. In Britain, the advent of these latter disciplines may have been accelerated by economic stringency and the perceived need to find ways of husbanding resources whose continued expansion could no longer be ensured.[2] In Sweden, by contrast, the driving forces behind new disciplinary involvement was provided by the recontouring of higher education that resulted from the U68 Commission (1968) and from the subsequent changes in administrative structure, patterns of governance, and in the relocation of administrative authority, inside a reform firmly grounded on the principle of integration.

Different disciplines, different paradigms

Thus the expansion in the number of contributing disciplines to the study of higher education is as spectacular as the changes in the system which they are engaged in studying. And no less remarkable in their variety have been the perspectives that these disciplines, in varying combinations, brought to bear on that same institution. The earlier historical scholarship tended to underwrite a cultural perspective on the university, casting it in the role of the seeedbed of cultivation, of scholarship, of learning for its own sake. The university, though the guardian of 'high culture' and the sensitivities, was, to be sure, in the world, but not part of it.[3]

The rise of educational planning in general and the economics of education in particular brought a fundamental shift in that institutional paradigm. It cast aside the metaphor of cultivation, and replaced it with the mechanistic concept of 'system'. The success and purpose of such a 'system' was to be judged by what might be termed its 'transformational capacity'. Such a concept had two meanings; first, its ability to adapt rapidly to increasing numbers of students; second, its capacity within a specific period to transform its student 'inputs' into suitably qualified 'outputs' to the labour market.[4] Not surprisingly, this paradigm which reduces higher education to an 'input'/output system, tends to emphasize the quantitative aspects, to centre around such issues as shaping the structures of higher education to the requirements of manpower needs, and to concentrate on conditions of access and policies of selection. It pays scant attention to the process or quality of education itself. Its prime concern is the functioning of higher education as an instrument for social engineering.

A third perspective is provided by the 'critical' sociology of education which has tended to concentrate on the alacrity or otherwise of the university to bring about greater equality of access to it between the various social classes. Or, as a correlative to this, it questions the function of higher education in upholding cultural – and by extension – social 'reproduction'.[5] Another theory perceives higher education as an incubator for new forms of stratification, identifying a new elite defined strictly in terms of educational achievement – the so-called 'new class' of knowledge experts.[6] Perhaps these perspectives reflect not so much the ambiquity of higher education's role as the rival perspectives within the discipline of sociology. Nevertheless, higher education cannot dismiss their impact.

More recent has been the application of systems or organisational analysis either as ways of optimising and rationalising academic decision-making – a hope that often turns out to be as vain as it is ambitious – or as a method for comparing functional differences and similarities in various countries without taking over much interest in their cultural, historical and political settings.

Finally, and perhaps most recent of all, has been the examination of higher education in its relation with the polity and the development of systems analysis. In this area, two main perspectives stand out. The first derives principally from the economics of education and tends to look upon higher education as a knowledge-producing 'engine' in relation to government priorities in science policy in general or research policy in particular. Its main preoccupation lies with analysis of the optimum conditions, structures and funding practices for the transmission and take-up of that knowledge – fundamental and applied – that is generated inside higher education and its subsequent use by government, industry or the local community. Obviously, decisions by governments to favour some forms of research as against others, to seek to guide it on the basis of a customer/contractor principle as enshrined in the Rothschild recommendations in Britain, in the rise of sectoral research in Sweden or the unveiling of the programme for research and science development in France associated with Jean-Pierre Chevènement as one time Minister of Technology and Industry, have wide ranging implications for the relationship between the state and higher education, whether directly or indirectly. The second perspective derives from political behaviour and more particularly from the behaviour of organisations and from the implementation of legislation. In its higher education setting, implementation theory reflects that shift of concern by governments from the act of reform itself to the problems associated with its execution, its delay or, in certain cases, its midnight burial.

The purpose of the report

Against this complex and still evolving field that is higher education, this report is placed. Its purpose is to provide an overview of Sweden's higher education research from a standpoint that is, at the same time comparative, international and historical. Within this overall context, however, its specific focus is upon such studies undertaken in Sweden and that have been sponsored by the National Board of Universities and Colleges (NBUC). A series of suggestions will be provided in the concluding section which will indicate possible areas for future research.

2

Salient values in Swedish society

'Progress, far from consisting in change, depends on retentiveness ... Those who cannot remember the past are condemned to fulfill it.'

George Sanayana, *The Life of Reason*, 1905–6

Introduction

Before going to the heart of our report, it seems essential to make some attempt at describing some of the principal values and assumptions that lie at the heart of Swedish society, and which have been paramount in determining the place of higher education in it. There are several reasons for so doing. The first of these is cultural. Outsiders carry their cultural impedimenta, assumptions, perceptions and values which, naturally, influence their observations. To the extent that these differ and, at the same time, give a different perspective on issues often taken for granted in the country one visits, they are often useful and valuable. And, conversely, those values that one takes for granted are very often put to new challenge by being thought remarkable by visitors from outside. Therefore, it is important in attempting to evaluate higher education research in Sweden, to place this in the context as well as our perceptions of that context of the values that may be said to underwrite such a programme.

The second reason for doing this is influenced by a disposition to think in

9

historical terms. Innumerable reviews by international organisations, like the techniques they utilise, are largely ahistorical. As such, they perpetuate the notion of 'value free' development as if human progress were not a continued conflict between values, interests and the choices that arise out of them. This approach to the historian – political, social or economic – is both mistaken and misleading. It is meaningless, for example, to discuss whether Swedish higher education is – or is not – centrally controlled without understanding the values, concerns and beliefs that have created this situation in the past and which persist in maintaining or modifying it in the present. To say that a system of administration is 'centralised' or to describe its government as 'democratic', is to answer no question at all. It merely states that such is the perception of the observer. In short, it raises more questions than it does provide answers.

The third reason for undertaking this excursion is that present practices are an unhelpful guide to the future. The policies of today and tomorrow are necessarily influenced by previous decisions. Higher education, just as the society in which it evolves, is both the victim and the victor of its past.[1] Finally, an historical dimension poses a warning that in any evaluative study and one based on institutional comparisons, there is the question of transferability. Measures that work in one country, as many constitutional draftsmen have found out, often undergo strange mutations when transplanted to another. As Dahllöf has noted in connexion with distance teaching in Australia and Sweden, sometimes this is due to physical factors such as population dispersal.[2] But no less relevant is the fact that the values acceptable in one context have less legitimacy and acceptance in another which is very often the fundamental reason for the failure in the first place. One example of immediate relevance to this report is the question of the proper relationship between the institutions of higher education and the State. There are many models and, moreover, their operational consequences are not fixed but alter over time.[3]

By contrast to the formal position of the Anglo American university, the Swedish university appears to have a low degree of institutional autonomy in respect of nominating its own decision-makers or deciding the activities of their component institutions.[4] This is *not* to say that Swedish universities enjoy less academic freedom – though some might make the point. It is simply to say that similar institutions often enshrine similar values in different ways in one country as compared to another. Why this is so is not *just* the result of different beliefs on such matters as the role of the state in higher education, the place of the university in social progress and the expression, through political decisions, of certain value convictions that tend to have more weight in some societies than in others. It is also the result of their particular history.

It would be impossible to analyze all those dimensions and subtleties that have contributed to what one might term *faute de mieux*, as the 'Swedish tradition' in policy making for higher education. One may concentrate profitably, however, on what appear to be its salient dimensions and which are inextricably linked with the Swedish political culture and national imperatives – some dating from as far back as the Seventeenth century, others of a twentieth century origin.

After consideration we identify what seem to us to be five particularly Swedish features of higher education policy of which some are taken for granted in Sweden but not necessarily elsewhere:

• The concept of the 'strong' state.
• The notion of 'Enhetlighet'.
• Equality in society.
• The positivist, rationalist style of policy-making.
• The practical versus the theoretical in higher education.

Let us look more closely at the meaning of these notions and values.

The concept of the 'strong' state

From the middle of the Seventeenth century, the Swedish university has been a direct instrument of the state, sometimes used to extend the principle of cultural uniformity, often employed to maintain the orthodoxy of religious belief. In the reign of Charles XI, for example, the university of Lund served as a direct instrument for the cultural and linguistic assimilation of the Southern part of the Scandinavian peninsular as a part of Sweden rather than of Denmark.[5] Furthermore, defence of theological orthodoxy – always important in a country with a state church – against the subversive beliefs of the Enlightenment served to emphasize the close relationship between states and theology faculty.[6] The same principle is reflected in the reforms which, between the years 1720 and 1770, attempted to create a curricular structure in line with the type of education required by the central government civil services.[7] Thus the idea of the university's role to serve the state is deeply embedded in the nation's history and continues as an expectation.

The importance of this development is three fold: first, because the setting up of formal rules and conditions governing entry examinations to central government civil service marks the beginning of the modern university; second, because it recognizes explicitly the principle of a meritocracy rather than hereditary privilege in the administration of a country; and third, because in Sweden this development tended to come earlier than in the rest of Europe. In Austria, the unequivocal subbordination of the university to the requirements of a naissant state bureaucracy was the work of Maria Theresa (1717–1780) and her son Joseph II (1741–1790)[8] whilst similar reforms in Prussia, associated with Alexander von Humboldt, and France with the setting up of the Imperial University, dated from 1809 and 1811 respectively.[9]

The development of the Swedish welfare state, on the other hand, seems to fall into three phases. The first lasted from 1932 until the end of the 1940's, the second from the early 1950's until the early seventies and the third from the early seventies until the present day. The first saw the laying down of the touchstone of the welfare state, concentrating principally on an active labour market policy aimed at eliminating unemployment; the development of housing subsidies to eradicate the grosser and more intolerable aspects of deprivation and the establishment of a child welfare provision, in part to tackle to roots of deprivation, in part to encourage an increased birthrate. Though delayed by the war, these policies were rapidly expanded in the immediate post war period, by major changes in the tax structure and the orientation of industry towards foreign export market. The second stage saw the implementation and expansions of these policies, which centred mainly on enhancing productive efficiency, the adjustment of the education system to the twin imperatives of social equality and the changing skill and occupational structure of society and, last but not least, the effective realisation of the principle 'from each according to his ability to each according to his needs'. The fruits of high productivity were re-distributed not only according to needs but also in keeping with the principle of solidarity.[10]

If such periods bore witness to the benefits of rational planning, open decision-making and consensus building, they also saw concomitant increases in centralisation. The third period may, by some at least, be characterised as a break up of consensus. Others, of a rather longer memory, will point out that the issues under discussion are less a break up of national solidarity, as the realisation that to a very large extent, the goals of the first reform period have been achieved. The question is really about the direction in which national consensus should tend. Should the principle of the strong state be extended further? Should rational planning and resource management be extended to cover the entire field of economic activity and bring it under popular control?[11] Or should some form of balance be struck between those tasks best performed by the state and those that permit personal commitment and activity within the various branches of the popular movements?[12] Yet, even the pleas made for the development of a market economy – in opposition to what some non Socialist parties see as the overmighty power of the state – show there is little disagreement over the need to maintain a state that is strategically strong in terms of economic and welfare policy. The call by the Liberal party for less regulation of industry, for example, still admits the right as well as the justice of maintaining the framework of direction in the hands of the state.[13] A socially directed market economy presents no challenge to the principle of a strong state. It merely believes – in the words of the physicist, Piet Hien, that 'a little bit less is more than enough'.

The construction of modern Sweden in the nineteenth and twentieth centuries rests on the conviction that it is the role of the state activity to advance liberty, equality and solidarity. The concept of a strong state acting as the prime economic regulator in the distribution of resources, whether in the form of an active employment policy, the development of comprehensive social security or housing is less a change in the notion of the state itself so much as a reorientation of its priorities. A leading Swedish political scientist has, for instance, recently argued, that the transition from monarchical authoritarianism to the modern welfare state in Sweden by passed, to a large extent, the state of bourgeois liberalism.[14] Thus, the question of whether social progress might be defined by the efforts of individuals working from below, as opposed to their agregation from above, has rarely been posed. Nor was the question widely debated as to whether the citizen owed loyalty and obediance to the state and its representatives rather than suspicion, and resistance in the face of its encroachment. One explanation for this is that the state, even in the period of monarchical authoritarianism, was not perceived to be oppressive in nature, a fact which may owe more to the difficulty of communication than to a commitment to enlightened monarchy.

Thus, the goal of political movements and, from the end of the 19th century the Social Democrats in particular was not to alter the nature of the state but rather to take it over the better to redirect its efforts in reshaping society and to use the instruments at its disposal to this end.

Direct control over the processes of production was not in the first intance a major issue, in part because it was held that the raising of living standards for all was better ensured by a policy of maintaining an independent private sector of industry whilst heavily taxing it to provide the resources.[15] In part also, because a considerable measure of control over production had been developed through the popular movements, consumers cooperatives, housing cooperatives, national health insurance, etc.

Historically, the 'strong state' in Sweden is justifyed by the need to protect the weak and to lessen the arbitrary power of elites – whether feudal, clerical, capitalist or bureaucratic because it stood as the only body in society with sufficient power to humanise and make more efficient the country's existing system of industrial capitalism.[16] Thus the Swedish state took over those responsibilities that had already been developed within the framework of the popular consumer movements expanding them through legislation. In other words, the strong state as developed by the Social Democrat party was justified as an expression of social progress developed from below within the popular movements to which the traditional apparatus of government was harnessed.

This is not to say that the modern Swedish university ever lacked either academic freedom or standing as a community of scholars. But it could not claim – as did the two Ancient English universities – to be an 'autonomous, property owning corporation'.[17] Its autonomy was subject to frequent royal interventions and inspections (formalised attendance lists at graduate seminars, duly certified by the professor were regularly despatched to Stockholm.[18] Its property owning did little more than underline a highly fragile economic base. Already by the end of the 19th century, government finance accounted for some 50 percent of the university budget. What this did mean, however, was the absence of any widely subscribed theory – let alone practice – by which the state could admit that the university enjoyed a regime of legal exception. In other words, because the university was both an institution and an instrument of state that latter was bound to exert those values on the university which the political interest had in turn inserted into the state. This was to have very specific consequences when the construction of the welfare state looked upon education *in toto* as a long term-strategic input to full-scale social reform.

The notion of 'Enhetlighet'

Studies on Swedish society accord major importance to its drive towards the attainment of equality.[19]

Leaving aside the complexities of this issue till later, there seem to us to be two main dimensions to the concept of equality in Swedish. Since both of them have considerable bearing on the context and the goals of Sweden's higher education policy, and to reflect the essence of society's values, it is important to draw the distinction between them. We have chosen to underline the difference by retaining the terms untranslated. These are 'Enhetlighet' and 'Jämlikhet'. If the latter may be understood as being 'equality before the law' between individuals or groups, the former is rather less easy of interpretation.

As one writer[20] has also pointed out, there is a difficulty in translating 'Enhetlighet' adequately into English. The difficulty is not so much etymological as related to political culture and administrative traditions that exist in both Britain and the United States. *Enhetlighet* involves the notion both of procedural uniformity and through it, of administrative equality. It endorses a concept of equality through administrative procedure better understood in the French Jacobin than in the British administrative tradition. Uniformity of administrative practice, procedure and by them, of provision are the guarantors as well as the legal and physical means by which a policy of 'Jämlikhet' (equality) is both manifested and upheld. Contrary to the overtones that such a notion has in the Anglo American culture – which are largely negative – *Enhetlighet* has a very positive quality that may embrace national and territorial unity (and by extension may therefore be seen as an earnest of both cultural assimilation and class solidarity). To revert to an example, used earlier, the University of Lund acted as an instrument of Enhetlighet over the earlier Danish provinces, assimilating them into the Swedish nation. In terms of education policy in general and more specifically higher education policy, it is this principle that justifies central control over the outer legislative framework, both budgetary and administratively. Its most concrete expression in recent times emerged in the U68 proposals for the creation of the comprehensive university, its structure, governance and organisation of studies.

In short, *Enhetlighet* may be seen in two perspectives: first, as an expression of the strong state acting to bring about equality through uniform and standardised provision; second, and by extension, as an example of rational planning in action.[21] As such, it is a general and essential element to the dynamic of Sweden's higher education policy.

Equality in society

If equality of individual opportunity in Sweden as elsewhere has been a constant theme in post-war education, its philosophic, psychological assumptions, its implications as also the policies based upon them, have altered considerably. There have been various typologies used to describe the varying interpretations, their social, educational and political consequences. Husén, for instance, has related this to the prevalent political ideologies of conservatism, liberalism and radicalism.[22] Neave, arguing from a standpoint of the history of ideas, identified four different strands: The predestinative, the redemptive, the dissenting and the sectarian interpretations.[23] Regardless of the differences in perspective, it is a fact that Swedish educational policy has been firmly predicated on the intimate conviction that greater access to knowledge is a moral obligation as well as a social and economic necessity. Changes in basic, secondary and higher education thus had a dual justification. It is important to underline the fact that changes in higher education were closely associated with reform in the secondary area – a feature found neither in British nor French educational reform in the Fifties and Sixties.[24] Tapping the reserves of ability could be looked upon as enhancing industrial and economic efficiency on the one hand and on the other as a means of creating a society 'strong' in its conception of implementation of social justice.

This is not to say that a similar dual justification was absent in other countries' higher education policy, though it is correct to say that it tended to take place later – in the Sixties rather than as in Sweden in the Forties and Fifties – and to emerge in different institutional forms. In Britain these twin imperatives – or rather their pale shade – underpinned the decision in 1966 to expand higher education through the setting up of 32 polytechnics. And in France, the same year saw the decision to implement the initial creation of what were to be 54 two-year University Institutes of Technology. But unlike Sweden, the policy of equality of opportunity was not allowed, structurally at least, to transform those institutions of higher education associated with the formation of the political elite.

In part, this different development springs from a major ethical shift in the definition of equality of opportunity in Sweden, in part from the concept of the goals of reform itself. As regards the ethical shift, from being concerned with the selection of *able* individuals from all social classes to persue education as far as their abilities would allow them, equality of opportunity assumed the status of a social good to be shared out amongst everybody on the premiss that everybody ought to obtain as much education as he or she was capable.[25] Such thinking underpinned, politically at least, the recontouring of Swedish higher education in 1977. It broadened the type of groups for whom such opportunity should be extended, to include women, regional and cultural minorities and members of the older generation, groups politically defined rather than defined primarily in relation to their cognitive ability.[26] As regards the concept of the reform, equality of opportunity was not seen, by the political authorities at least, as something confined to those in receipt of education. It was, as we have suggested earlier, an important strategic aspect of a wider social transformation. Educational change was not, as one might suggest in the case of Britain, France and Germany, intended as a substitute for social change, confining and limiting those pressures to the education system. Rather, it was seen as a process for accelerating development – for forcing the pace – in the economy, in the labour market and in the home.[27] For this reason, no educational institution and *a fortiori* the university could be exempted from its part of contributing towards greater equality of social and political opportunity.

The positivist rationalist style of policy-making

Swedish political culture has been described as rationalistic, deliberative, open and consensual in its decision-making.[28] In an earlier article, focussed mainly on secondary education, we suggested that an outstanding feature of Research and Development in Sweden, was apparent conformity to the hypothetico-deductive model.[29] Even though recent studies have tended to be more circumspect, suggesting that this approach appears less valid in the implementative and evaluative than at the decision-making stage[30] it still has considerable significance. This is because the earliest studies of scale into higher education were carried out within the framework of, or sponsored by, Royal Commissions enquiring into the condition of that institution. Research on higher education was thus a contribution to, as well as a part of, that rationalistic tradition. Conversely, the rationalistic tradition has had no little influence upon the methodologies of some of the social sciences.[31] It has, then, moulded certain disciplinary cultures in academia, to such an extent that they stand apart, both in their focus of interest as well as their general approach, from similar disciplines elsewhere. In essence, rationality in Swedish political culture is both procedural and empirical. Some have classified it as in the positivist tradition of Auguste Comte.[32]

Positivism may be seen both as a particular ideology criticising traditionalist values implied in a government's actions and as a critique of the techniques of government. It proposes the alternative method that such policies as modern governments have to administer or initiate, are better grounded and the action more sensitive in consequence, if based on the use of empirical knowledge gathered through statistical enquiry. Its rationality lies in the assumption that it is sufficient merely to confront men with the objective truth, represented by such empirical fact-finding for them to recognise the error of their ways. They would subsequently reach agreement in the light of this self evident truth.[33] The harnessing of empirical enquiry to the work undertaken by Swedish Royal Commissions may be said to reflect this sort of procedural rationality. Indeed, the integration of research into the workings of Royal Commissions itself constitutes a very specific item in the Swedish administrative style. Contrast this, for a moment, with equivalent action in British Commissions of Enquiry. As one British commentator wrote, '. . . the epitome in Britain is to set up a Commission of enquiry made up largely of distinguished practitioners in the chosen policy field with a token academic who may or may not be invited by his colleagues to organise research'.[34] In short, the positivist approach in the United Kingdom has never become the conventional wisdom, while in Sweden, though the positivist approach has achieved that status, it is currently being re-appreciated.

Recently, there has been a revival of a discussion on the proper contribution of research to policy-making. It is suggested that, in fact, the use of research to determine both policy-options and policy implementations may well be rather more limited than it once appeared to be the case. We will deal with this issue later in Chapter Three of this report. Yet, irrespective of which interpretation is more correct in this matter, research continues to provide a means through which consensus can be attained. Moreover, it forms a significant part in the formal process of Swedish government policy-making.

In the United States, it has become fashionable to refer to the 'engineering model'[35] of policy making and there is some importation of these theories into Sweden – but more among academics than practitioners.

Swedish positivist rationalist policy making in practice seems to have developed on indigenous lines. Essentially, this follows a sequential procedure along the lines 1,establishment of commission; 2,review of problem; 3,research/investigatory activity; 4, presentation of report to the responsible minister; 5,circulation of report to all interested popular movements and parties; 6,presentation by government to Parliament of a bill based on the Commission's recommendations and views expressed in stage 5; 7,parliamentary decision.[36]

Another fact of the characteristically Swedish and positivist approach to policy-making, lies in the close association between government and the nature of the social sciences taught in the universities. One observer has noted that amongst the outstanding features of the social sciences generally and in particular, the development of sociology in Sweden has been their empirical orientation, their emphasis on measurement and on the quantitative approach with much stress placed upon methodological accuracy and conceptual clarity.[37] The weight attached to studying phenomena that lend themselves to quantification and to measurement, to the notion that the social sciences may use the procedures of the natural sciences has been the result of two processes, Scace argues. The first is the use of social science data for administrative purposes: the second is said to be a mistrut of the speculative, a reserve about constructing grand theories of social development. These may be said to be the major characteristics of the rationalist tradition in the Swedish social sciences. When added to the fact that, almost without exception, empirical data gathering is national rather than local, underties a macro rather than a micro approach in those disciplines, one begins to appreciate how the social sciences have themselves adhered to an intellectual edition of *Enhetlighet* and in turn been influenced by it.

The practical versus the theoretical in higher education

In July 1977, as part of the reorganisation of higher education, under-graduate studies were regrouped into five professionally oriented sectors. These were:
1 The technical sector
2 The administrative, economic and social welfare sector
3 The medical and para-medical sector
4 The teaching sector
5 The cultural and information sector.

The notion that higher education should be 'vocational' in the sense that its studies should develop skills and aptitudes that lead on to employment is not, of course, new. Indeed, in that sense, the traditional faculties of the medieval university – Law, Theology, Philosophy and Medicine – were highly vocational. Nor is the supplementary issue – which type of knowledge is more conductive to social and individual progress – the theoretical or the practical, education for cultivation or training in the concerns of the real world – without long historical precedent. On the contrary the debate is perennial, with advocates for the modern rationalist party being supported by Bacon, Descartes and the *philosophes* of Enlightenment.

The development of nineteenth century industry in Western Europe served to underline these tensions. The response of governments lay broadly speaking in two directions. They might set up new institutions – apart from the traditional university. Alternatively, they might incorporate the new 'disciplines' within the academic framework of the university, with the result that their development would owe more to the values and dynamics of the university world than to the real world they were meant to serve.[38]

If the 'professionalisation' or academic and theoretical bias of certain knowledge traditions, which at their origin were practical was and is a European wide phenomenon, one recent ideological and political response to this process has seemed to be uniquely Swedish. The reasons for this are deeply rooted in the culture of Swedish society and since they form the tap root of that current of thought which led to the 'vocationalisation' of higher education in the late Seventies, it is important to take them into account.

In Sweden, as in other Scandinavian countries – Denmark being a prime example – there is a strong tradition or an organised, popular culture running parallel and outside the official education system.[39] Such movements were instrumental in demanding not only extended educational facilities for their members and thereby symbolising a 'democratic demand' for education in general. They also looked to the state to organise education held to be of practical value to their members. Indeed, the origins of today's Centre party in Sweden – the former Agrarian party – may be traced in part, back to the movement by Southern Sweden's farmers calling for better technical education for the farming community. This juxtaposition of a numerically powerful, popular body of interest groups on the one hand and a politically influential elite, identified by its command over the official institutions of knowledge, served to add a further dimension to the notion of 'professionalisation' or 'scientification' of knowledge. These two processes became symbolic – at least in the minds of Social Democrats – of the indesirability of alienation of knowledge from society, and a warning that the democracy of the ballot box could be offset by a self-reproducing aristocracy of intellect.

To this ideological interpretation was added another dimension derived from the economic imperative. The structure of the historic university faculties and the knowledge alignment they represent does not always 'mesh' with changes in and the types of skills demanded by society. These mechanisms for matching educationally transmitted skills with vocational outlets and opportunities have been perennially under review since the start of the Sixties. The fineness of the 'tuning' is a particularly Swedish phenomenon in government – higher education relationships.

Conclusion

In Sweden, the economic justification for 'vocationalisation' in higher education had slightly different overtones than elsewhere in Western Europe. For although the commitment to equality of educational opportunity could be seen as a complement to the expansion of highly qualified manpower – a dual motivation found in other countries too – in Sweden it contained another dimension besides: namely, the wish to bring higher education nearer to society by reorienting its content away from the theoretical and more towards the practical. Nor, one might add, is Sweden any longer alone in so doing. Current debate in France over the future higher education guideline law (*Loi d'orientation*) to replace that of 1968, has devoted considerable attention to the question of restructuring undergraduate studies around specific occupational sectors rather than around the traditional academic disciplines. In the United States as well, the drive towards the practical and the vocational in higher education is no less marked in recent times.[40]

Nevertheless, if there seem to be certain trends towards the 'convergence thesis' by which education in one country appears to be moving on a convergent course with counterparts elsewhere, the motivations behind the apparent similarity of outcomes differ widely. The priorities expressed in public debate just as the research that is fostered as a result of such discussion, are largely determined by the values and convictions of a given society, as well as by the way in which that society believes it *possible* to move from 'what is' to 'what ought to be'. Whatever course policy takes, it is bounded by values, implicit or explicit, which in turn are rooted in the history of a particular country. Swedish society displays a high confidence, comparatively speaking, to set and achieve long-terms goals in public policy.

3 Research on higher education in Sweden

The reasonable man adapts himself to the world, the unreasonable one persists in trying to adapt the world to himself. Therefore all progress depends on the unreasonable man.

George Bernard Shaw, preface to *Man and Superman* (Penguin 1982, p 260).

An administrative history of a Programme

The Research on higher education programme was founded in 1971 by the then Office of the Chancellor of the Swedish Universities (UKÄ). The setting up of the programme itself was not novel, though the extension of a permanent research instrument, specialising in the study of *higher education*, was. Already in 1962, the Riksdag set aside a special budgetary allocation for R&D inside the National Board of Education, to be devoted to the development of school research.[1]

The extension of the R&D principle to the field of higher education study must be seen, however, against a rather broader background of the evolution in Swedish Research and Development policy generally. The late Sixties and early Seventies saw an enormous growth of what has been termed the 'Sectoral principle' in scientific research. This development, the origins of which can be traced back as far as the 1940's in Sweden with the setting up of the Technological Research Council[2] assumed a particular significance in the Seventies. The guiding force behind this move, which came rather earlier to Sweden than to other countries,[3] was for government authorities to fund and develop research aimed at enhancing their policy-making capacity. Broadly speaking, sectoral research may be said to correspond to the 'customer-contractor' principle enunciated in Britain by the Rothschild Report in 1971. It involves the application of fundamental scientific research to solving problems falling within the purlieu of a specific government agency – housing, defence, health or, in this case, higher education. Looked at from the specific viewpoint of this agency, the application of such a principle may be seen as the higher education counterpart to the drive towards 'sectoralising' research within Swedish government authorities generally. It sought to bring higher education closer to the perceived needs of society. Higher education's own research and development activities may be looked upon as having a monitoring role as well as monitoring a future-oriented approach to this same imperative. The former responsibility is exercised by the follow-up programme of the NBUC, set up in 1976.[4] Only the broader research programme carried out in the universities is the direct concern of this report. In short, we are concerned here with the 'research' side of the NBUC's work, rather than with the 'development side'.

If the rise of the sectoral principle provides the general backdrop against which the Research Programme may be set, there are other more specific factors acting inside higher education itself. Prime amongst them was the recommendation of the expert committee on the development of university teaching in 1970. It suggested that more weight be attached to research and development both at central and local level, especially in the area of staff development.[5] In 1982, the total sum devoted to this purpose was in the region of Sw cr 14,000,000, most of which is employed for the inservice training of university staff and the remainder being assigned to what may be termed institutional research – for example, follow up studies of graduating students.

The need for a specific programme for research and studies of higher education on a permanent basis sprang in part from the considerable amount of research commissioned by the U68 committee. This Commission involved a wide range of research enquiries touching upon such matters as higher education and the labour market, rate of return studies, forms of governance and the regionalisation of higher education. Since the Chancellor's Office was already acting as a *de facto* coordinating agency for this work, there was much to be said to placing higher education research on a permanent footing. Finally, the then Chancellor, Hans Löwbeer, had recently transferred from the National Board of Education and was fully convinced of the need to develop within the context of *higher education* those research and development facilities already extant in the National Board of Education. Moreover these arrangements coincided with the strongly held Swedish value of higher education as a 'good' that should be fairly, rather than unequally apportioned.

The programme as a whole

The research programme on higher education has its secretariat in the Research and Development Unit of the National Board of Universities and Colleges (NBUC). This unit forms one of the divisions of permanent staff. The Programme's original purpose was two fold: first to commission research from university departments, as an input for policy development within the central agency; second, to foster research of a more theoretical and fundamental nature as a contribution to the long-term development of higher education. It was, in the earlier stage of its history, seen as part of the central decision-making organisation of higher education. Its primary task was to increase the stock of knowledge on what may be termed 'the outer frames' of higher education activities that were controlled and planned at a political level.[6] Over the past few years and most particularly since the formal decentralisation of university decision-making that followed the reorganisation of higher education in July 1977, the long term perspective has come to predominate. Initially, however, the programme was heir to much of the research carried out within the framework of, or deriving from, the concerns generated by U68. In this sense, then, the research programme may be seen as a continuation of that traditional model of research and policy development that has characterised Swedish education in general for the past 40 years. This model has sometimes been termed the Research-development-diffusion model or alternatively, the Engineering model of research and policy-making. Having grown up within the framework of *ad hoc* royal commissions, the consequence of establishing a research and development unit was to give it a permanent funding base without, initially, altering it.

If higher education research within the then Office of the Chancellor was, to a considerable extent, an established practice transferred from the National School Board, it became very quickly apparent, both as regards procedures, steering and the type of discipline involved, that the higher education programme was subject to its own internal dynamic. It began to diverge considerably from the practices laid down in the National Board of Education. First amongst these was a different approach to steering research which, in the context of the National School Board, was often very closely defined by the central authority. It has been argued, for instance, that one reason for this is that university based research does not easily lend itself to close direction. As a statement of general principle, this may be true, though it is a principle that is observed more in the breach than in the application, as much of the literature on science policy in Sweden has observed.[7] More influential by far in determining the delicacy of the external steering was the rather more subtle purpose which central administrators saw the programme fulfilling namely, to act as a vehicle of dialogue between centre and periphery, between administration and university. The building up of confidence between the two parties was seen as rather more important – if only to foster a new style of alternative and critical research – than enforcing adhesion to the paths of righteousness by whip, knout and admonition. No less important was the need to attract high quality researchers into the study of higher education, which served to reinforce voluntary self-restraint by the central authorities.

Finally, there was the question of the participating disciplines. Here, the issue assumed a dual character in part arising from the way in which the purpose of U68 was interpreted, and in part, arising from the nature of higher education studies. They do not exclude any discipline from participation. And though one specific subject area may, at a certain moment, tend to have the lion's share of funding, this reflects not just changes in funding priorities and current concerns of the administration, but also the energy with which different disciplines and individuals submit their applications. As regards the former, U68 was construed as a review of the total function of higher education in society. Simply to deal with what was seen as a social reform from within the relatively narrow disciplinary bounds of – say – the educational sciences was not deemed appropriate.[8] This was further reinforced, at the top echalons of the central authority, by the feeling that the contribution of paedagogics to policy development, had not proven altogether satisfactory.

It is unclear when the decision to place less emphasis upon the educational sciences was reached, if indeed it was reached as a clear cut decision at all. Some officials regarded this disciplinary shift as explicit from the time the research and development unit was first established. Others have seen it as a more protracted process.[9]

Equally significant was the gradual change of emphasis in the programme's stated objectives. At first, the main concern seems to have been to ensure that research in higher education – of whatever mode, action oriented or fundamental – was of an international standard. By 1977, the accent was placed on relatively long-term research, concentrating on 'theoretically deduced priorities' as a supplement to action or development activities.[10] The following year, the explicit linkage between commissioned research and policy development, vanished. 'The programme' its preamble stated, 'is not directly tied to current reform work'. It was, rather, concerned with a number of questions of a fundamental importance to higher education ... as a whole'.[11] Three years later, its objectives had become even more broad-ranging, with its principal aim being 'to enhance *our insight* (our italics) concerning the role of higher education and research in society and our understanding of the conditions in which higher education is best able to accomplish its mission'.[12]

Change in the research paradigm

The importance of this shift may be said to reside in three areas. First, the added weight accorded to long term strategic research reflects the general concern felt in other spheres – the Council for Planning and Coordination of Research, the Royal Commission on Research Collaboration which reported in 1980 and last, but not least, the Swedish Parliament itself. Second, because it showed that the research programme was prepared to draw on conclusions in some of its commissioned research to modify its objectives in that light. Third, and perhaps of most historic significance, such change in objectives covers a fundamental shift in the research paradigm on which the programme was initially founded.

The historic paradigm on which the research relationship had built up in the area of education revolved, as was suggested earlier, around the Research-development-Diffusion of 'linear engineering model'. This, irrespective of the contribution research might have upon influencing the option taken up, had been the basis on which ad hoc research in Sweden rested since the time of the Wicksell Jerneman Commission on graduate unemployment in 1933.[13]

Why this should be so lies as much in the area of the policy process to which research was reckoned to contribute, as in the theory of research itself. Up to and, in certain instances, beyond U68, research as an aspect of policy formulation tended to concentrate on the input side. Certainly, this involved evaluation of previous reforms and to that extent may also be said to have turned around the 'output' side as well. But it is nevertheless evident that from around 1976, higher education research tended to concentrate more on the consequences of policy decisions, on the implementation of reform measures taken previously and thus, increasingly on the intentions of policy makers and their effects as perceived by those involved in other parts of society or the system of higher education itself.

The theory which tends to dominate American analyses of the policy process – and which was imported into Sweden – is that the role research may play in decision-making is at one and the same time, more limited and more complex than the notion of rational sequentiality implied in the so called 'Engineering model'.[14] Rather than acting as a direct contribution to policy-making, research is held to influence the way decision-makers view the particular problem under review and to alter, delicately, the manner in which they conceptualise issues. The influence of research is seen as an indirect permeation – a light to lighten the Gentiles and to enlighten administrators. Research then, influences through 'illumination', through providing insight – a term that the programme took over as one of its explicit objectives thereby espousing that same 'enlightenment model' of research and policy interaction that it had called upon its researchers to investigate.[15]

Illumination and enlightenment, however, may equally be construed as a two way process and as such, this paradigm shift may also be viewed as strengthening the implicit aims of the programme. Prime amongst these, following a report written by Martin Trow in 1975,[16] was the aim of using the programme as a vehicle both to sponsor and consolidate a community of scholars in the field of higher education. A subsequent evaluation from within that community has suggested this is well on the way to being achieved.[17] This aspect of the programme will be dealt with later in this Chapter. Suffice it here to note that, if it is very unusual for a central government agency to seek to create *ex nihilo* a scholarly community, the initiative in itself is to be praised. One should, at the same time, remember, however, that this development is fully within the Swedish tradition of linking academic research in the social sciences to the needs of government.[18] It would, of course, be incorrect to say that the association of economics, sociology and psychology *entre autres* to the ad hoc investigations of government commissions *created* those communities. But it did have the effect of considerably enhancing their prestige and thus, in no small measure, consolidating them inside academia.

In parallel to this aim ran a second, namely to persuade those of the 'grass roots' in Swedish society to take a more active part in the policy debate. This aim is particularly interesting in view of the greater emphasis placed on the decentralisation of decision making in higher education as a result of the 1977 reforms. From this standpoint, such an aim may be said to represent an extension into the domain of research of the principle of self determination that underwrote the broader change in higher education.

Budget

If these were the evolving aims of the programme, how were they realised? Since its inception, it has launched over 90 projects spread across 12 disciplines in the field of both social sciences and humanities. In addition, some 30 conferences and meetings to discuss specific topics took place within its framework, in addition to two international conferences of major scope.[19] These activities belie the modest financial resources at its disposal. Over the three years from 1980, the programme's budget has remained constant at Sw Cr 2,000,000 despite considerable inflation over this period.

Taken over twelve fiscal years of the programme's existence, the amount accruing to it as a percentage of the total sum devoted to Research and Development for higher education has tended to diminish from 19 percent of the 1971 budget to 11 percent for the years 1980 to 1982 inclusive. Hence, expanding the scope of the programme has had to contend with rather strict financial limitations.

Before going into the budgetary distribution between disciplines, it is important to note the way in which the programme classifies its main research areas. In 1973, three general areas of interest were specified. These were:

1 The role of higher education in society
2 Higher Education as a system, governance and structure
3 Environment and working methods of teaching.

This grouping corresponded broadly with the interests and issues aroused by the work of the U 68 Committee. To them was added a fourth – environment and working methods of research in 1973 and, four years later, a fifth comprising the topic R&D Organisation and Planning. They were deliberately designed to be flexible and to accomodate to the interests and concerns not merely of government but also of researchers. They were not conceived as hard and fast categories. In consequence, much of the research that formally falls under one head might equally and with no less justification have been grouped in another. In 1982, a further realignment in the programme content took place which cominbed areas 3 and 5 of the Programme.[20] This gave rise to four generic groupings.[21] They are:

1 The Role of Higher Education in Society
2 The Organisation of Higher Education
3 The Research Function
4 The Educational Function.

The changing focus of interests emerges clearly when one examines the proportion of the budget assigned to each topic area, on the basis of three four year periods up to 1982. Over the twelve years of its existence, the importance of the Role of Higher Education in Society has tended to remain very much on a par inside the programme. It accounted for 38 percent of the total allocation, though predictions for the five years from 1984–1989 suggest this will drop to around 30 percent. The 'Organisation of Higher Education' saw a doubling in its share from 16 percent in the period 1971–1974 to reach 30 percent of the total budget between 1979–1982. Most marked is the upward rise in fortune of the Research Function area. From 2 percent in 1971–1974 it now stands at 19 percent of the budget for the past four years and will rise, it is predicted, to gather into itself a quarter of the financial allocations for the five years up to 1989. The Education Function which accounted for a handsome 43 percent in 1971–1974, fell constantly to reach 13 percent in the last four years of the programmes operation. Its allocation for the period from 1984 to 1989 will probably amount around 15 percent.[22]

Obviously, these topic areas are strongly aligned with the specific subject disciplines. Hence, it is hardly surprising to note that the disciplines of Education and Psychology which retained the lion's share – 70 percent – of the first four year period and still attracted 52 percent between 1979 and 1982, though still remaining the largest single area of allocation in 1984 to 1989, will take away some 35 percent of predicted budget. Falling too are Business Economics, Economics, Geography and Economic History after a high point of 16 percent over the period 1975–1978 vanished from 1979 onwards and will continue to shine by their absence. On the other hand, Political Science has found itself a steady niche with 18 percent of the budget in 1979–1982 and can look forward to around 20 percent of the predicted resources for the five year period after 1984. By contrast, the rise of what might be termed the 'value sciences' – Philosophy, History, the History of Ideas and the Theory of Science – is outstanding. From a mere 2 percent of the budget between 1971–1974, they will take up a predicted 30 percent of the 1984–1989 budget.[23]

Qualitative change

Changes in the budgetary profile of the various disciplines are a pale statistical reflection of surprising alterations in the focus of the programme. If it began its life by studying such technocratic matters as the 'effenciency' and 'productivity' of higher education and by investigating what one might term the 'official dimension' of that same institution – the organisations of studies, siting of new establishments, and administrative procedures – it has developed, moving from the quantitative to the qualitative from the public life of university to the private lives of those professions to which it contributes, from the organisation of culture to the cultures of organisations, sub-professions.[24] From examining the outer frames susceptible to immediate legislative or administrative intervention, the main focus of research on higher education has moved over to investigate the more subtle internal processes of higher education as well as the perceptions of them by the various elements of the higher education constituency – students, staff and administration – both towards the consequences of reform as[25] well as the more general and long term effects of higher education as a process of 'enculturation'.[26]

The expansion of the contributary disciplines and thus of their several perspectives have undoubtedly recast the light in which the university system was itself perceived. Rather than being the recipient and the executor of reform decreed from without, it was soon recognised and certainly by administrators within the NBUC as having its own internal cultures, different knowledge traditions which themselves affected the way that reform was interpreted.[27] This initial perception seems to have affected the development of the programme itself – an apparent example of the proposition that research cannot forecast its future development. One effect of research has been to give new recognition to the legitimacy of certain disciplinary cultures inside the university – which hitherto had often been regarded as sectarian interests acting contrary to the political imperative of institutional reform – and to examine the way their value systems had developed.[28] No less significant was the recognition that disciplines other than the quantitative social sciences were capable of making important contributions to the study of policy development, and to expanding the knowledge base on which government might care to draw in the future. Such knowledge was not, of necessity, limited to areas of immediate application in fields of technological, industrial or administrative demands coming from without higher education (which the principle of sectoralisation tended increasingly to emphasise). It could also be used to lay bare some of the implicit assumptions made by government in launching those programmes.[29]

In short, the addition of certain subject fields, more particularly, the History of Ideas, the theory of Science and policy analysis to the gamut of disciplines hitherto included in the programme altered the intellectual perspective to the relationship between government agencies, higher education and public policy. Prior to bringing the 'value sciences' into the research programme on higher education, much of the research tended to take for granted the frames and objectives that government ascribed to higher education policy. Its purpose was, rather to examine how far such objectives had or had not been met, to point out possible lacunae that later administrative action might correct. The advent of 'critical' research not only tended to question the *frames* of the policy but the *values* that underlay it as well.[30]

Steering and commissioning research in higher education

The transition from research in an instrumental mode, 'customer defined' to a more wide ranging exploratory approach had repercussions on the relationship not merely between the programme and its sponsoring agency but also with other fund-granting bodies as well. To some, the emergence of the programme as an intellectual 'broad church' was a desirable development. It recognised the need to counter the administrative uniformity imposed on higher education by the 1977 reforms with a greater degree of 'cultural pluralism' in the type of research undertaken.[31] To others, the departure from research defined heavily by the commissioning department was questionable, not least because the type of enquiry emerging from the programme appeared too broadranging and too complex to contribute directly to the policy-review process. Such research, it was argued, might better be funded by the Research Councils which were the main source for fundamental enquiry.[32]

What such criticism overlooked was the strategic purpose of relatively free-ranging enquiry inside the programme. This, as has been pointed out earlier, formed part of a strategy to build up a coherent research community, specialising in higher education. To have moved the funding over to the Research Councils though perhaps more logical from a strictly organisational standpoint, would have returned the area of Research into higher education to a situation often found in Britain and France, where it exists as a relatively dispersed area of activity by individual researchers. Second, it failed to take adequately into account the fact that such development takes time. And, finally, such criticism implied that the programme itself had moved over to fulfilling a Research Council function – that is, funding academic research – rather than steering research deemed useful to the commissioning agency. This latter problem is, of course not unique to higher education. The concern of administrators lest commissioned research come to reflect the preoccupations and internal values of academia rather than the priorities of government is a tension that is ever present in sectorally driven research, as British studies have shown.[33]

The question of how accomodation is reached between the research community's concept of 'relevance in research' and the type of investigations the commissioning agency deems significant is always a delicate task. From its outset the Research programme adopted a comparatively sophisticated approach to the question of commissioning, steering and monitoring research. This consisted of three separate elements, only one of which was officially entrusted with the task of evaluating research proposals. This comprised two Advisory groups, the first composed of practitioners and planners, chosen from amongst university vicechancellors (Rectors) administrators within higher education, including officials from the National Board. The second is composed of professors representing the various disciplinary areas participating in the programme. In 1982, their numbers stood at six and five respectively.[34] The remit of both groups is to examine research submissions. The first works within the context of the type of contribution the individual proposal might make to policy planning and to the political objectives of the higher education sector. The second works within a very different perspective and concentrates on such matters as the academic credibility, methodology, design, and scholarly quality. In February and March of each year, submissions are sent out to two separate researchers, one in the discipline in which the project is located and the second from a non-related field to get two opinions. These assessments are laid before the two advisory groups along with the project itself. In addition each member of the two advisory groups is asked to give his personal assessment for each project. After separate meetings of the two Advisory Groups, a final joint meeting takes place usually in early April when recommendations from both sides are discussed and the individual submissions rank-ordered within each of the four priority areas. Interviews with those participating in this procedure suggest that agreement on suitable projects is relatively high and that those recommended by one group are often the same as those supported by the other. In the event of formal divergence, the practice is, it would appear, to defer to the recommendation of the academic advisory group.[35]

If the criteria for assessment laid down for outside assessors are similar to those given by the Research Councils, the programme does depart from the usual practice of those bodies by insisting on external opinions outside the discipline.

In fact, the formal procedure for research submissions is only the start of a long and delicate process of search and identification both of problem areas, potential projects and researchers that takes place in the various conferences, problem area discussions and seminars that go on throughout the year. Their importance is not merely in the opportunity provided for potential projects to be discussed and negotiated in a non-official manner. They also allow representatives of higher education policy to state their concerns to researchers prior to the latter submitting their projects. At another level which is not less important to researchers, they provide occasions for feedback and problem discussions which loom very large in the programme and thus have both a manifest and a latent function. They serve to review possible future developments and at the same time allow both researchers and practitioners to find ways of marrying together the priorities of the latter and the particular interests of the former. In fine, occasions such as these are very much part of the process of 'interactive steering' between government and academia that has in recent years, come to be an outstanding feature of the higher education research programme.

That this is favourably received emerged strongly from the interviews held with various university academics engaged on studies within the Research programme. Lack of advise from the commissioning body, uncertainty as to what the exact implications of the type of research they were being asked to do, were characteristics that many attributed to *other* larger funding bodies. As one researcher said:

> 'We know what they (the NBUC) think and they know what we think and they help us to get into contact with other researchers. With the other body, you are left to yourself. You get no feedback. You have no evaluation of your research.'

It can, of course, be argued that the closer and sustained personal interest shown by officials in the programme is both at matter of personal commitment and a function of the comparatively small number of projects involved. The broader the scope of the programme, the more difficult it may be to maintain this level of involvement. The testing time of the Research programme would be, then, if its budget were suddenly to expand, thereby putting such a burden on its central administration that it found itself obliged to formalise those forms of discussion, negotiation, advice and suggestion which, up to the present, have been on the basis of unofficial collaboration or guidance. In essence, the strength of the programme lies in the constant interplay between general policy-makers, decision-makers concerned with development and researchers in which the latter have relatively easy access to the two former groups, both on a formal basis at colloquies and on an informal basis through personal and direct contact. Yet, more striking by far to outsiders is the intense loyalty felt by researchers towards the programme as a whole though, naturally each would like to see his or her particular area receive a rather larger share of the programme funds than is at present possible. This is a healthy sign. It is, after all, well-known that the one feature researchers share with Oliver Twist is their shameless asking for 'More'.

4 The research on higher education programme: an analysis of selected projects

As soon as questions of will or decision or reason or choices of action arise, human science is at a loss.

Noam Chomsky, interview March 30, 1978 BBC TV.

Introduction

In this Chapter we turn our attention to an analysis of certain selected projects which may be said to represent the main areas of research found in the Research on higher education programme.

As has already been pointed out the programme invites application from scholars regardless of discipline or locality. In addition, it actively sollicits wide participation. The pattern of projects nevertheless shows a pre-eminence of interest – as might be expected – from researchers in the social science and certain of the humanities areas. How then, might one categorise the projects in order to analyse their content and orientation?

Methods of analysis

One method, adopted by this programme is to divide current projects into five problem areas. These are:

- The role of higher education in society
- The organisation of higher education
- The conditions and potentialities of research
- The conditions and potentialities of education
- R&D organisation and planning

There are, of course, numerous other methods one of which might, conceivably be by identifying the contributing disciplines: philosophy, history, the history of ideas, business economics, economics, sociology, psychology, education, political science and public administration.

The task of categorisation was sidestepped initially by the need to find out more about the individual projects. The method used in this report was to take an overview from the documentation available with a view to selecting particular projects to discuss them in more detail with the researchers involved with them. This had the advantage both of gaining information of a qualitative nature and of eliciting views from individuals with widely differing perspectives on the higher education research programme as a whole. In short, it has beeen possible to see how the programme appears from the standpoint of the research unit and the university as well as from the centre. In addition, comments have been elicited from administrators and public figures within Swedish affairs who have, at one time or another, been connected with research into higher education.

We have found that the projects of which a particular study has been made for this evaluatory report, fell into the following five groups. They do not coincide with – although they resemble – the programme's 'problem oriented' classification. The classification used to analyse some of the programme's studies, may be seen as a type of continuum: at one end is a focus on the study of the individual student in higher education. At the other are projects which examine the relationship between higher education, research, government and society. The categories used in this report are:

- Learning studies (Learning about learning)
- Disciplines, knowledge traditions and values
- The organisation of higher education
- Policy analysis and government interaction with higher education
- Higher education and research policy (Research about research)

Learning Studies (Learning about learning)

The experience of higher education upon the cognitive development, values and professional orientation of individual students is amongst the earliest problems to tax the interest of researchers in higher education. In the United States, cognitive development was a major issue in the Sixties both on its own and also as an instrument to seek out optimal teaching methods. There is some reason to think that if the extension of these two concerns to Europe drew on a slightly different context, both owed much to the conviction that traditional teaching methods in higher education were no longer suited to changes in higher education itself. In Europe, the investigation of study and learning methods of students drew much of its motivation from the rise of mass higher education. Methods suited to an elite were less relevant in a situation where student aims, abilities and inclinations appeared rather more broad ranging, it was felt. In part also, considerable influence was exercised by the ephemeral promise held out by educational technology that it could enhance individual student learning. The combination of these two elements gave rise to the blooming of a thousand 'Staff development' programmes and to a sub field known as *Hochschuldidaktik* in German speaking countries.

The fundamental purpose of *Hochschuldidaktik* involved the manipulation both of content, subject boundaries and teaching methods in an effort to optimise cognitive gain. To this extent, then, it remains fully in keeping with the quantitative approach to personal development. Rarely, if at all, did it set itself the task of investigating *what* students understood.

The particular perspective which seeks to elucidate those concepts of learning held by students and the characteristics of the 'learning contexts' as experienced by students has been developed principally, by researchers at the Göteborg Department of Educational Research. Described by its principle protagonist, Ference Marton, as 'phenomenographic', its main purpose is to describe the world as perceived by the learner.[1] Originally, Marton had been engaged on the Learning and Study Skills project, commissioned in the late Sixties as part of the research sponsored by the UPU Committee. If the investigation started off as a direct input to contemporary debate on university teaching methods, the interests of the Göteborg group evolved very quickly towards basic and fundamental research and more specifically, towards the type of learning strategy used by students in mastering a specific corpus of knowledge.[2]

Marton distinguished between two types of approach used by students – the surface and the deep level – which, he argued, were qualitatively different from one another. The former led to a mastery of the particular disciplinary vocabulary, though not necessarily to understanding the essential concepts contained in it. The latter, by contrast, did entail a firm grasp of the essential and fundamental concepts underlying the technical linguistics of presentation. By investigating the individual's perceptions of the process of learning itself, Marton reached two major conclusions; first, that the strategy employed by the learner – surface or deep level – constituted the decisive factor in non-verbatim learning;[3] second, that the subject context was as highly significant as the study technique. In effect, the Göteborg school argued that general learning skills should be seen as intrinsic to the study of subject content.[4]

This was a highly important finding. It suggested that the so called general theories of learning developed by the *Hochschuldidaktiker* in particular, were not capable of effective application. Insofar as study skills led to a deep-level understanding, their development was both subject context and discipline bound.[5]

It is claimed that the phenomenographic approach yields original insights into the different academic disciplines. Since it is applied to describing the individual's perceptions of the world around him, it can also be employed not merely to a specific field of learning and cognition, but, by slightly altering the perspective, may be made to reveal students' perceptions of a particular academic discipline or their notions towards a possible future profession. Investigations which began in the field of cognitive development in Economics,[6] Education[7] and mechanical Engineering[8] have now been extended to assess the experience of higher education upon the individual's perceptions of working life. Thus, having begun as an 'investigation into the grammar of academic thought', as one interviewee termed it, – an enquiry into the *enduring* effects of learning in higher education – the same perspective is now being applied to examining what might be seen as the individual's initiation into professional life and, from there, on into the dynamics of professional socialisation. At the present time, this investigation is relatively limited. It involves in-depth interviewing with a relatively restricted number of students in medicine, technology, psychology and economics. However, the particular approach involved should ensure that it is a significant complement enhancing the more sociologically and historically based studies on the evolution of professional occupations.

If the Göteborg group has, as its main concern, cognitive development and the long term concomitants of what might be called 'academic intelligence'[9] the project at Umeå University, though relying on a similar phenomenographic technique, has a slightly different emphasis. Its aim is to investigate the nature of ideological transmission through the education system and the implications this has for students' 'images of the world'. The central construct of this project is a concept of 'personal representation' (*Vorstellung*). The way the individual represents the world to himself acts as the controlling factor against which the impact of higher education on the individual may be evaluated as part of the *process* of cultural and social reproduction. It is held that those 'personal representations' the individual makes for himself are based on systems of knowledge about the surrounding world. Such systems of knowledge are assumed to undergo change of a qualitative nature as a result of students being exposed to new forms of knowledge and different values permeating higher education.

The aim of the Umeå project is to examine one of the central functions of higher education – namely, its social and cultural reproduction.[10] Though the Umeå and the Göteborg projects are working closely together, the former takes a different perspective from the latter. Whereas the Göteborg group began with the classical canons of developmental psychology, the Umeå study derives from radical sociology of education.

Its methodology is to monitor the progress of students drawn from medicine, technology, psychology and economics. These disciplines have been chosen on the grounds that they play a key role in Swedish society and, consequently, have high social standing.[11] Like the Göteborg studies, this investigation is both theory generating as well as theory testing. Researchers justify this on the grounds that the qualitative aspect of student perceptions in this domain is, to all intents and purposes, virgin territory. Its goal is said to be the examination and analysis of that process of ideological conditioning contained in the different courses in higher education. Other aspects included are the image future members of the liberal professions have of them prior to entering. This is examined in the light of the self-image a given profession conveys through its major professional journals. Students perceptions of the social structure, already investigated, have thrown up differences between the social model endorsed by students in engineering and that accepted by students in economics.[12] Other perceptions tested relate to the hierachy of the work-place and students' attitudes when faced with certain topical – and value-laden – issues: for example, 'The distribution of wealth in Sweden'.

The LONG project is a notable departure from the rather more well-established models of evaluating institutional impact through either achievement tests or attitude measurement which, in the past, have tended to overlook the more long-term qualitative effects of higher education. The LONG project may be viewed from a series of different perspectives: as an attempt to break out of the quantitative method of evaluation; as a means of relating the effects of a particular institution to its broader cultural and social context; or as an empirically based exploration of one of the main theories in the field of the sociology of education.[13]

Evaluation

From an external viewpoint, these two projects hold a particular significance in the context of the higher education research programme, on the grounds that theoretically and empirically, they are uniquely Swedish. Those involved in them have been supported by the programme since its earliest days. Such *continued* support not only allows teams to build up their expertise. It also permitted them to develop methods and concepts which have contributed to other scholarly work in Britain[14] and in Australia[15] though less in the United States. It has opened up a valuable perspective on the interaction between higher education upon the individual and, through him, on society generally. How far this may contribute immediately to discussions concerning future priorities in higher education is a delicate matter. Few can doubt, however, that it has provided an additional and highly sensitive insight into the effects of higher education upon the personal, moral and cognitive development of its principle client group – students.

Disciplines, knowledge traditions and values

To many, the concept of an 'academic discipline' as a vehicle for passing on and developing a corpus of knowledge that is consistant and cohesive – this is the Ark of higher education's convenant with Society. To others, the idea of a 'discipline' is itself to be questioned on grounds of its 'relevance' for contemporary society (the utility argument) or on grounds that it is instrumental in maintaining an established political order through control over access to knowledge or the manner in which its contents are presented (the idealistic argument). Irrespective of whether one deprecates or supports the concept, studies on student 'enculturation' assume that the course or study-line represents different values, varying techniques of training and a particular ethos that vary substantially from one to another. All 'disciplines', then, may be said to constitute different 'knowledge traditions' – some being located inside formal academia, others only recently brought in, some long established, others in a painful state of becoming. Amongst the former, one may refer to the medieval disciplines of theology, law and medicine. Amongst the latter are those associated variously with the phenomenal growth in scientific advance – nuclear physics or molecular biology – or with the growth in the functions of the modern state, such as the newer branches of welfare economics, public administration or social work.[16]

The growth in the number of 'disciplines' is directly tied with the expansion of higher education and the expansion of higher education, in its turn, has very largely been connected with the need to train and educate personnel for the new 'caring' industries – social work, nursing, guidance, counselling and, not least, education itself. Until the reforms of 1977, many of these 'para-professional' activities took place outside the university *stricto sensu*. Their consequent incorporation inside the comprehensive university has given rise to considerable discussion both of the place of the 'newer disciplines' as well as their relationship with the more 'traditional' fields of university study. Though some studies into the growth of certain Humanities disciplines have been long-term enquiries, undertaken prior to the 1977 reform of Swedish higher education, the bulk of those falling into this category appear to be direct responses to issues arising out of the public debate. That scholarly enquiry should be stimulated by public controversy is no reflection on the quality of research. Indeed, it is arguable that a more profound analysis of those issues of concern to citizens is, itself, a desirable contribution of research to knowledge in the community at large. But such research often has a very particular context to which to respond and this, in its turn, demands some preliminary analysis of the points of controversy.

If formally, the 1977 reforms abolished the historic structure of 'disciplines' for undergraduate studies, it broached certain fundamental questions not merely about the relationship between those activities hitherto central to the university and those previously associated with specialist training in *non-university* centres. It also raised such essential points as the place of professional status that arose out of such knowledge and finally, the manner in which professions sought to gain control over the nature of that knowledge they regard as essential to them. Alongside the question of the relationship between academic disciplines, knowledge traditions and professional values ran another of particular acuity since it was seen by some as constituting the heart of the 1977 reforms – namely the parity of esteem between what were held to be practical, community-based knowledge traditions and the theoretical, academically respectable 'subject areas'.[17] This latter aspect, as we have suggested earlier[18] was especially important in the Swedish context – though it is also present elsewhere – since it rekindled a long-standing issue between the theoretical and the practical traditions that are evergreen in Swedish educational and political controversy.[19]

An examination of the studies sponsored by the higher education research programme which correspond to the 'culture of disciplines' (knowledge tradition being a rather broader concept) reveals three main fields; those dealing with the internal cultural dynamic of the particular discipline formally defined[20], those focussing on disciplinary cultures as instruments leading to the 'professionalisation' or, alternatively, the 'scientification' of knowledge: those which take as their primary variable the profession itself – or sub-profession, as the case may be – as a case study to investigate the way in which knowledge is monopolised, defined or transmuted by contending interests inside the naissant 'profession'.

Odén's study of the development of graduate education in Sweden from 1890 to 1975 may be said to be typical of the first approach. It investigated four 'established' disciplinary fields: history, cultural geography, political science and economic history. Based on classical historical sources, archive material dealing with the type of topics discussed in graduate seminars, an analysis of thesis titles and, through them, the rise and fall of the various schools of historical thought over the previous 85 years, the purpose of this enquiry was three fold: first, to examine the way in which scholars in these fields were trained; second, the transmission and perpetuation of particular schools of thought across student generations; and third, the contents of graduate education.

The study reveals that in the case of Humanities a very specific notion of scholarly training and cultural transmission was involved. This took the starting point that historical judgement is not a matter of training or of technical competence alone. Rather, it requires long-term and sustained immersion in the subject so that the transmission of the discipline's essential values relies both on a hermeneutic approach but also on a species of intellectual apprenticeship and craftsmanship. The acquisition of judgement is therefore part and parcel of the individual's maturing as well as the assimilation of particular perspectives by direct contact with mature scholars.[21] Odén's investigation is essentially, internalist from two points of view: first, because it studies the development of these disciplines from inside the university world, though it also relates changes in the hegemony of the various schools of thought inside these disciplines to wider political and social developments; and, second, because, it is an historical enquiry conducted by an historian. This latter point sets this study apart from others insofar as it involves an exponent of a particular discipline examining it within the criteria and canons of scholarship of her substantive field.

No less significant at least from the standpoint of one specific discipline – history – is the fact that Odén's enquiry reveals the extent to which externally imposed reform may, in certain circumstances, be destructive of even the most ancient of academic knowledge traditions. The effects of the U63 reform which, in curtailing the length of study time, also presumed that the process of intellectual socialisation was similar between the natural sciences, the social sciences and the humanities was instrumental in undermining the humanities' craft/apprenticeship model of 'enculturation'.[22]

The perspective of 'disciplinary cultures' seen as exemplars of the mechanism of 'scientification' or the 'professionalisation' of knowledge has been pursued by Elzinga, Bärmark and Wallén. Taking the emergence of nursing care as a field of university based research as an illustration of this process, they examine the relationship between practice-based craft from which it developed, and the theory-based 'discipline' into which it is evolving.[23] Particularly close attention was paid to two aspects which, in effect, are a direct reflection of the 1977 Reform: the link between research and working life and the link between research and the new study lines that the reform introduced. The perspective employed derives in the main from the theory of science, the sociology of science and the sociology of knowledge within an interdisciplinary framework. The project set out to interview key personnel in the nursing profession – and more specifically, those who had taken or were sitting for the Ph.D degree in this area, practitioners responsible for training on the grounds that such persons would represent both 'traditions' – practice-based and theoretically oriented. However, the examination of a profession in transition and of the various knowledge paradigms contained in the scientific and practitioner elements shows the highly theoretical orientation of this project. It is not directed towards the study of this 'profession' as such, so much as the knowledge paradigms that its changed status inside higher education appears to entail. To the extent that it focusses on the relationships between knowledge attitudes, ideologies and the organisational forms which the

1977 Reform introduced, it may be seen as both a *post hoc evalution* of some of the consequences of that reform as well as a contribution to understanding the finer nuances involved in the 'scientification' of knowledge at the moment when, conceivably, it is taking place in this specific field. Seen from this latter angle, this project represents an interesting example of the way an area of study oriented towards practicality assumes the elements that later may coalesce into a full-blown disciplinary culture. The relationship between the emergence of disciplinary cultures and the scientification of knowledge is also examined by Esbjorn Johansson within the context of the historical development and training in the social work 'profession'.[24] Though complementary to the previous study, Johansson's enquiry appears to be conducted within the framework of the sociology of the professions and has a substantial historical element. It traces the development of social work training since 1910. His point of departure has been heavily influenced by the model of 'alternative' knowledge traditions drawn up by Bergendal.[25]

The social work profession can be seen as paradigmatic in the sense that it represents in very concrete form many of the ambitions and goals contained in the 1977 reforms – the links with working life, the need to develop a research base and, at the same time, a tension arising out of conflicts inside the profession itself. Johansson argues that social work constitutes effectively a specific sub-culture which, whilst not having the formal trappings of an academic discipline, nevertheless is endowed with a separate identity, specific training methods, clearly defined links with working life and, most significant of all, its own knowledge base. This might be said to apply equally to the nursing profession. But there are important differences in emphasis between to two investigations. While Elzinga, Bärmark and Wallén regard the process of 'scientification' in the nursing field as a vehicle for testing and elaborating certain aspects of the theory of science and the modus operandi of particular forms of knowledge production, Johansson takes a reverse approach: namely, the consequence in the change of 'knowledge production' from a practical to a theoretical base upon the development of a specific profession. In part this difference in approach springs not merely from the different disciplinary perspectives involved – though Elzinga et alii claim to operate from an interdisciplinary standpoint – but also from the fact that the two 'professional cultures' are at very different stages in their development and have, therefore, important differences in the degree of legitimacy they enjoy. Hence, it is not surprising that whilst both face the possibility that their incorporation into higher education will result in an enhanced theoretical bias in the type of knowledge they are expected to convey, the possible consequences would appear markedly different. Incorporation may well alter qualitatively knowledge traditions in nursing, but it would seem also to offer the opportunity of conferring additional legitimacy upon this field. Johansson, on the contrary, is concerned with the possible effect on a hitherto self-standing training programme of its incorporation into the realigned occupational structures that form the basis of undergraduate education. And, to this extent, the prospect of formal incorporation into higher education may well break up an established professional subject 'culture'.

If Esbjorn Johansson's enquiry involved an established 'professional culture', Jan Erik Johansson examined the knowledge traditions in an emerging and non established occupational group – pre school teachers. Though sharing certain features with both the nursing and the social work studies – namely the consequences of the 1977 Reform upon this specific occupational group – J. E. Johansson employed a methodology that combined history with the phenomenographic approach. It is also more concerned with the dynamics of professional development inside the education system, cleaving thereby to the empirical rather than as an elaboration of the theoretical. The purpose of this study is to trace the development of child care in Sweden during the 20th century and then to analyse the changes involved through the perceptions of pre-school teachers. Essentially, his aim is to identify changes in the type of knowledge which result from an occupation evolving out of a craft and gradually attaining the status of a semi-profession.

Broadly speaking, the three projects analysed have, as a constant theme running through them, the tensions that emerge inside 'professional' and 'disciplinary' cultures or value systems when change is imposed on them from without by a combination of economic and political forces. No less important, however, in the evolution from craft to discipline or profession is the role of contending groups inside the fraternity seeking to redefine the content of knowledge to their best interests.

The role of such groups inside the medical profession formed the basis of the historical exploration carried out by Ingemar Nilsson. In Sweden, as in other European countries, the area of medical practice divided into two clearly separate 'knowledge cultures' – the practical and empirical re-presented by the barber surgeons and the theoretical upheld by medical doctors.[27]

Nilsson's study is both historical and comparative, tracing the two traditions back to medieval times and across four contries – England, France, Germany and Scandinavia. It examines the differences between two traditions in such matters as their training, recruitment, social status and financial conditions. Nilsson was especially concerned to lay bare the precise mechanisms that brought about changes in professional organisa-tion and the gradual integration of different knowledge forms. It has been commonly held that changes in medical knowledge or in scientific advance generally served to redefine professional specialisation. Rather more important, Nilsson proposed, is the use to which such new knowledge is put and this, in turn requires a rather closer examination of the social and institutional context in which the various types of medical practitioner evolved. Crucial to the development of any profession is its ability to obtain an institutional base from which to promulgate its particular form of training with the backing of public authorities. Nilsson analyses this aspect in terms of the conflict in the early 19th century between doctors and surgeons over the future of the Caroline Institute at Stockholm. Briefly put, the issue was whether medical training should conform to the theoretical model in vogue at Uppsala or the more practice based orientation then current at Stockholm.[28]

Nilsson's work, carried out within the Department of the History of Ideas at Göteborg, may be seen as a combination of medical history, sociology of knowledge, and the sociology of organisations. More explicitly than other projects concerned with the evolution of either knowledge traditions or discipline cultures, his may be seen as a direct contribution to contemporary debates – more specifically the future of the medical profession, particularly with the rise of social medicine and the consequent changes in medical education that this would appear to warrant.[29]

Evaluation

With the exception of Birgitta Odén's study which dealt with graduate education in Sweden, the projects analysed in this section appear to be commissioned as a direct consequence of the public debate that centred around varying and often conflicting interpretations about the long term purpose of the 1977 reform of the Swedish university. And, seen from this single standpoint, they have provided an important and long term perspective to issues which that reform threw into sharp relief. The value of such studies may be judged, however, from several points of view. First, they have conferred a broader background to the fundamental points of controversy – the relationship between the practical versus the theoretical, the history of professions, some based in university, others not, the mechanisms that underlie the definition of disciplines and the value systems they uphold. Second, those that are historically-based have shown that the controversy aroused by the creation of an integrated system of higher education is not just a passing thing of the moment but encapsulates matters of enduring concern that have been 'solved' in different ways in the past and yet retain their importance in contemporary society. The tension between knowledge traditions is now, and has been over the past two centuries, a topic of abiding concern intimately linked with the rise of the 'professional society'. Third, they provide – though perhaps on an *ex post facto* basis – a solid historical framework for an innovation implemented under the imperatives of educational planning.

There are relatively few studies on the comprehensive university that seek to place its priorities and their effects within the context of the 'disciplines' contained in it. There has, for instance, been considerable work on the theoretical and practical links between the comprehensive university and the labour market in West Germany.[30] In Britain, though the concept of the comprehensive university has been discussed by Robin Pedley,[31] the implications for different 'discipline cultures' remained untackled.

Though all the enquiries mentioned in this section deal with knowledge traditions from different perspectives, there is a marked difference between those conducted by practitioners of the discipline concerned and those undertaken from the standpoint of a third party remaining outside it. The former appear to concentrate on the implications for the particular discipline or profession, the latter on the rather wider ranging implications for the development of particular theories of knowledge development and transmission. There is much to be said for both approaches especially since the latter tends to contain a multidisciplinary perspective that seems to yield interesting insights. But one may question whether such investigations might not profit from the active participation in the research of at least one member of the profession or discipline under scrutiny.

That said, it is nevertheless very unusual for public policy research – which, in the Swedish context, the research on higher education programme is – to bring in the humanities in general and the historical analogue more specifically, as a means of providing new insights to the long-term perspective. Contemporary educational development has tended to be dominated by what one English writer has termed the 'tyranny of the present'.[32] Hence, at a time when long term strategic considerations are being developed in other domains – energy policy, science research – it is appropriate that research on higher education should seek to extend the long range principle. Inspired looking forward demands inspired looking back!

The organisation of higher education

If 'disciplinary cultures' stand at the heart of the enterprise of higher education, increasing attention has been paid over the past decade to the way in which these are formally organised into basic teaching units, the type of decisions taken at the various levels of organisation, the decision-making 'style' – whether hierarchical or collegiate – and the relationships of power between the interlocking levels – department, faculty, senate – that constitute the 'visible university'.[33]

The motives behind this move are many; the wish to see to what extent historic structures of decision-making and governance are compatible with the demands of economic efficiency; the twin and ever-present imperatives of public accountability on the one hand and participation on the other and the ways in which they may – or, alternatively, may not – be inserted into structures already in place; the degree to which such internal structures may adapt to change either internally developed or externally imposed. Essentially all these themes have a common inspiration and derive from the same central development – namely, the increasing centrality of higher education as an instrument of public policy. To some, the study of the organisation and decision-making structure of higher education reflects the fact that higher education itself has become subject to bureaucratic rationality.[34] To others, such bureaucratic rationality is itself a symptom of the changing balance of power between academia and administration to the detriment of the former.[35]

Irrespective of the values endorsed vis à vis this phenomenon, the formal organisation of the university is the crossing point between what Trow called the 'private life of higher education' and the public domain.[36] Hence such organisation represents the outer, formal expression of the interior life and values of particular 'disciplines' or, seen from the outside, stands as the inner limits to which public and government decisions penetrate and are discussed. Such bodies act in short as a species of 'interface' where public policy and interior values meet, clash and are sometimes mutated beyond all recognition. In terms of medieval political theory, they may be regarded as those points at which the descending hierarchy of public policy meets the ascending hierarchy of academia.

The studies undertaken within the framework of the Research programme into the inner organisation of higher education and into the values and attitudes held by its denizens, show an interesting dynamic. Early investigations tended to be highly empirical and related to a specific task, often associated with the U68 commission on university reform. Carried out within the perspective of business administration or organisation and management studies, their task was to explore the range of options that reorganisation of higher education might consider. Alternatively, their target involved examining the adaptive capacity of the university as a preliminary to overall integration of different sectors of higher education into an integrated system.[37] Other studies, though fully within the same mode, examined the potential of different forms of internal organisation to meet student demand in highly specific circumstances. For instance, could regionally-based demand be better met by organisational patterns based on adult education institutes or was it best served by a broadly based model founded on institutes affiliated to the university?[38] The characteristic of such early studies was their concentration on the development of new systems or administrative units or, alternatively, their adaptive capacity seen from a *systemic* perspective. They were essentially, taken up with investigating the outer frame of such organisations as contributions to planned change developed from above. Or, to put it another way, their concern lay with the descending hierarchy of public decision-making rather than with the ascending hierarchy of the community of scholars.

Such a standpoint, however useful for examining such issues as the overall public control of higher education, was rather less powerful in elucidating the exact role played by decision-making or staff attitudes at departmental level. What, in short, were the elements that gave strength to the voice of scholarly interests? Was the power of this latter, in effect, altered in any way by the advent of new patterns of participation and public control? What were the factors that contributed to its power, its influence, in short, its relative autonomy inside the university?[39]

Lane, working from a Public Administration perspective, undertook a series of investigations into the nature of departmental and university autonomy from a comparative standpoint.[40] His conclusion was that the 1977 reforms in effect increased the degree of autonomy in the areas of educational content and departmental organisation, but at the same time had considerably reduced what he termed 'autokephaly'. This latter may be restated as the ability of the university to appoint its leading representatives. Government appointment of Rectors and local government nominations to the local governing board, he argued, stood as a significant weakening of the strength of 'autokephaly' in its formal sense.[41] Whether such changes affected the inner workings at departmental level was a different matter. In an earlier analysis of the type of decisions taken in the senate of Umeå university over the ten years from 1964 to 1974, Lane argued that changes in management techniques and budgetting procedures did little to alter the essential dominance of the department in university decision-making.[42] The power of the ascending academic hierarchy resided firmly at the base which consisted of a series of relatively uncoordinated units whose members were nevertheless, united in perceiving the university in the same manner.

Lane's suggestion that academic power follows archaic corporatist or guild models is interesting from a number of points of view. First, because the finding was broadly similar to those reached in other studies carried out in Britain[43] and Italy.[44] Second, because it received further, though backhanded confirmation, through other studies, some of which took a systems approach to examine the obstacles to university innovation at a departmental level,[45] others which took a policy analysis approach to the problem of vocationalising higher education.[46] Powerful though the department might be, both as a unit of decision-making and as the key to academic excellence, its functions of research and education could still be undermined by a reinforcement of the powers accruing to the descending hierarchy of administration. Symptomatic of this latter phenomenon, Lane argued, was the increasing burden of administration and the process of bureaucratisation which was continually reinforced throughout the Seventies.[47] This shift in the balance of power is not, of course, limited to Sweden, but may be seen in countries as disparate as Switzerland,[48] West Germany[49] and the Netherlands.[50]

Their examination of the tensions between the two hierarchies led Lane and his collaborators in two directions: first and more theoretical, was to challenge the relevance of some of the models of organisational change applied elsewhere in public administration.[51] The second was to examine the values and attitudes of academics towards the 1977 reform. This latter can, of course, be seen from two standpoints: either as a Swedish version of the examination of the structures and values of the academic profession undertaken in Britain by Halsey and Trow[52] or as an exploration of the value systems operant inside academia which provide intellectual cohesion across the monadic chaos of university departments.[53]

If Lane was concerned with the changing nature of the contemporary relationship between external public policy and internal attitudes and response within the 'private domain' of academe, Svensson was rather more taken up with the historic dynamic of university development. His three volume thesis on the history of the Swedish university from 1470 to the present day, may be said to represent an interesting departure fom the established tradition of examining university reform from the perspective of changes in structure and organisation alone.[54]

As a sociologist working within the framework of an historical undertaking Svensson sought to combine an institutional perspective on the internal dynamic of the university's development with the broader aspects of societal change taking place *extra muros*. Amongst the elements that made up his internal institutional ecology were the formal machinery of decision-making, hierarchical relationships, the growth of administrative constellations. Changes in the cognitive content and the function of the university in relation to its surroundings were also included. Amongst the elements that constituted Svensson's external ecology were the development of the economy and the mode of production, shifts in the type of labour market to which university trained knowledge applied, and, finally, the relationship of the university to the state.[55]

Working within the Weberian tradition of sociology, with subsequent modifications from theories of the Frankfurt school, Svensson saw university development not merely as an expression of increasing bureaucratic rationality but also as an instrument through which various forms of knowledge evolved and were made to serve the interests of professional and intellectual groups in their broader societal struggle for autonomy, control and security.[56] In volume III which examined the period from the 1870's through to the 1970's, he argued that reforms in the Sixties and Seventies brought about a further transition. The university, he suggested, moved from being a technical–bureaucratic instrument of state to becoming a more directly political instrument.[57] Like Lane, he concluded that this process paradoxically, strengthened the bureaucratic administration in so doing.

The politicisation of the university's role and function in Swedish society is an important development and one touched upon by other investigations to be analysed later. Essentially, such politicisation involves the intervention of interests which, historically, were not aligned to the 'value allocating' bodies in society whose position the university legitimated. Amongst the more traditional are the law, medicine, theology, the central civil service and, in some states, though by no means all, the military.[58] The significant feature of these groups is their ability to perpetuate their group professional standing in the form of social reproduction. This Svensson touched upon in his examination of inter-generational mobility amongst students at Lund during the late 17th and early 18th centuries, though within the context of individual family mobility. As certain of Svensson's critics have pointed out, the enduring historical phenomenon lies not with the individual but the professional groupings.[59] From this angle, the politicisation of the Swedish university may be seen as the concomitant of new groups seeking the same historic advantages that the university conferred. If this is the case, then Svensson's conclusions about the emancipatory role of today's higher education system should perhaps be subject to historical caution. What may appear as a qualitative change in a linear development of that institution can equally be seen as a particular stage in a cyclical process.

Evaluation
Studies dealing with the organisation of higher education have tended to focus on the university as a relatively self-contained entity, responding to pressures from without. It is interesting to note, however, the qualitative change in the emphases of these investigations falling into this category. From being studies of specific application to an immediate administrative requirement, they have rapidly assumed a theoretical foundation.

Here one should distinguish between those studies seeking to apply a theoretical perspective developed elsewhere to explain Swedish issues and those which, using Swedish material, seek to modify such general theories or to propose alternative models held to be more powerful in Swedish circumstances. Broadly speaking, Svensson's undertaking may be said to correspond to the former and Lane's concept of a public administration model applied to the relationship between administration and organisational development within the Swedish university, may be said to correspond to the latter.[60] This difference is especially important. For whilst it might be seen as relevant to know to what extent developments in the organisational issues of Swedish higher education are in keeping with or depart from similar matters elsewhere, there is a wealth of difference between the *importation* of scholarly theory and its *exportation*. It is the difference between keeping abreast of the state of the art and actually contributing to the advancement of its outer limits. This is not to say that pioneering and scholarly work depends always on inventing one's own theories. That would be to deny the essence of the Republic of Letters. It is merely to point out that the use of theories developed in one country in a specific historical context are not necessarily nor easily transposable to other countries and other epocs.

Policy analysis and government interaction with higher education

The relationship of the university as educator of society's intellectuals to government – whether the Prince, the State or local 'notables' – has always been a matter of delicacy. This is no less the case in present day Sweden than it has ever been in Europe generally. It is therefore worthwhile exploring this phenomenon historically before examining the research which relates to the next two sections.

If the status of the university has changed from that of a private corporation[61] to becoming a major purveyor of trained and educated manpower, this has been almost universally associated with the rise of the centralized nation state. Whether in Spain of the early Bourbons, Austria under Maria Theresa and Joseph II, France under Napoleon I or Prussia under the influence of Humboldt, this proposition holds true.[62] The emergence of the modern European university was the direct product of policies of state intervention. This is not to say that theories about the proper limits to such policies were absent. On the contrary, they can be traced back as far as Marsiluis of Padua in the 15th century, to Kant,[63] Humboldt,[64] down to that arch exponent of non interventionism, Mark Pattison, who, as Rector of Lincoln College, Oxford stoutly defended the property rights of his college first and the scholarship of academe as an incidental second.[65]

The difference between state intervention in the past and its present form lies in the fact that prior to the Second World War, such interventions tended to be episodic, limited to a specific single aspect, for example, ratifying the status of a particular establishment or, confirming senior appointments. Since then, state intervention has expanded in scope and in its sustained nature. Such matters as regulating student numbers, re-defining the structure of higher education, laying down conditions of access, defining the criteria for student selection, redistributing power between the constituent elements – students, professorate, staff, representatives of the public interests at local or national level – drawing up new forms of governance, tighter control over budgetary matters – these are the everyday stuff of the contemporary state's part in higher education.[66]

The emergence of a system of close government involvement was perhaps seen earlier in Sweden than elsewhere in Western Europe. Nevertheless, the drive to exercise control and oversight and, in the Seventies the determination to set down objectives and norms of efficiency is clear throughout Western Europe. Such determination received its symbolic expression in the creation of separate ministries for higher education in Austria, Spain, France (though subsequently rescinded by the government of M. Mauroy), Portugal, the reform of the NBUC in Sweden in 1976 and the waning of the powers of the University Grants Committee in Britain.[67]

Such growth in direct state intervention has, naturally, attracted the research interest of those with academic backgrounds in government, in political science or in policy analysis who perceived higher education as a connected sub-field of their discipline. Such a development is not confined to Sweden and may be seen as a generic event.[68] The advent of these disciplines into the field of higher education brought about a major change in perspective in that domain. Attention now concentrated on the mechanisms of government bearing down on higher education, on their organisation in relation to this latter, their policy procedures, styles of operating. Thus higher education itself is perceived as an example of public policy operations. Whereas previously studies in higher education tended on balance, to assume a university centric perspective (cf. supra Ch. One) in which government action was seen as an external variable, now the standpoint shifted firmly to being administration centric and the university found itself placed as an external variable in the process of elaborating and implementing policy. In fine, academic attention moved to the study of the descending administrative hierarchy and its perception of higher education as an 'instrument' of its policy.

One Swedish study within this overall perspective, examines higher education policies within three countries, Britain, France and Sweden. Its interest in policy-making styles led the author to identifying six dimensions: policy change, centralism, level of consultation, openness in decision-making, level of conflict and the formal mechanism of policy deliberation.[69] Despite the increasing politicisation of the relationship between government and higher education – a theme taken up in closer detail in the Swedish context by Lindensjö[70] – higher education matters did not in these countries occupy a central place in national politics on a continuing basis.

Rather, Premfors argued, higher education figures as part of what he termed subsystem politics. This particular location left considerable opportunity both for elites and within such elites, certain portal person-ages, to exercise a disproportionate influence in policy-making. In examining the relationship between central government administration and academia from the standpoint of the effects it might have upon the process of policy implementation, Premfors also provided added insight into the question of the interlinking between the government adminstrative hierarchy and the ascending academic hierarchy. He identified some of the differences in priority, and differences in the criteria for judging the performance of higher education from the standpoint of both academics and administrators. If policy-makers were more preoccupied with those aspects of higher education that lent themselves to quantification – student numbers, social class background, levels of attainment and qualification – academics if left to themselves were more concerned with the content and the quality of what took place inside individual establishments and 'show little interest in the broad social and economic functions of higher education'.

Differences in perception between government and academia were also examined within the framework of a case-study on the implementation of the 25/5 scheme by Lillemor Kim. Kim noted the tendency for government decision-makers to emphasise organisational aspects of higher education reform to the neglect of other, no less significant obstacles of a qualitative nature such as individual's attitudes and 'life situations'. Solutions chosen on a bureaucratic basis, she suggested, may not be correct when seen in another perspective. One major critique of Swedish reform, Kim argued must be that insufficient account was taken of different values and goal conflicts when drawing up policy.[71]

In revealing the rift between policy-makers and academics and between policies as formulated from the centre and their subsequent emergence at the operational level, both Premfors and Kim applied to higher education an older issue in contemporary political science – namely the apparent paradox between the growing power of state intervention to affect the course of public institutions and the seeming disagregation in the *processes* by which it does so.[72]

Pushing his examination into the relationship between government and higher education policy development, Premfors developed his analysis further. In a series of articles, he investigated some of the accepted frames of Swedish policy making, in higher education – its centralised planning and administration, its uniformity and stress on social equality, the radical reform of structures and its rationalisatic procedures of policy formula-tion.[73] The strength of these policies is considerable, so much so that a change in government in 1976 did not, essentially alter the decision to carry on with reform.[74] Thus political debate about the future of higher education, he suggested, continued largely to be conducted within them rather than about them. In a further study into the genesis of the 1977 reforms, Premfors analysed more precisely what might be termed the anatomy of consensus about the social values that this reform incarnated.[75]

But what reality could one attribute to the notion that the way decision-making procedures inside the formal mechanism of research and review, in fact subscribed to the image of rationality they enjoyed? If rationality in decision-making might be the *end product* did the *process itself* correspond to the same canons? Taking the *ad hoc* Royal Commissions as quintessential of the text book process of decision making in Swedish public administration, Premfors' study reached quite the contrary conclusion. The Royal Commissions could not be counted as examples of neutral technocratic enquiry. Rather they served as a forum of exchange for different interest groups. Nor, he concluded, did objective social research act as a substitute for political negotiation in these commissions. Social research – as might have been expected – served largely as ammunition for the various interested parties to lay their hands on and interpret as best fitted their special cause.[76]

If the political ecology of the relationship between state and higher education is infinitely more exotic and complex when one focusses on the process of policy development rather than merely on the end of policy, no less important are the ideological assumptions that often underpin it. Lindensjö examined the genesis of the U68 university reforms in the light of three dimensions: the technocratic aspect, the intervention aspect and the politicisation of policy-making.[77] Working within a sociological framework developed by the third generation of the Frankfurt school[78] Lindensjo's interest lay in the process by which some options were taken on board and others rejected in public policy. What his study showed were the factors contributing to the erosion of the technocratic dimension in planned educational change. The notion that long-term policy could adequately be formulated by experts, professional planners and central administration staff as a 'value free' technical exercise was itself dependent on a high degree of political consensus and a relatively low level of conflict.[79]

Although departing from a different analytical standpoint, his conclusions were in some degree complementary to those of Premfors. The technocratic assumption, Lindensjö believed, might have served usefully to shield planning decisions from the profane, but could not overcome the fact that there still existed an inner forum for political conflict and interest-related negotiations. These studies indicate that the erosion of the technocratic assumption about higher education policy began when certain groups that had been part of the reforming coalition in conjunction with the central administration during the Sixties, notably students, moved into opposition. The rise of participation involving other groups than those traditionally associated with policy-making in higher education plus the determination by elected parliamentarians that higher education should be more firmly under their oversight came as a fundamental challenge to policy-making carried out by experts and central planners.[80]

The realignment in the constellation of forces acting in the area of higher education policy-making led Lindensjö to suggest that two main models could be postulated the first incorporating centralisation and the technocratic imperative; the second, identified by decentralisation and the principle of participation.[81] Nor was Lindensjö very hopeful that the coexistence of these two policy development subsystems would serve to overcome the more intractable obstacles to planning. Though complementary, there is some indication that they are also self-cancelling to the extent that the implementation of measures developed within the former seems to generate difficulties that can only be resolved by recourse to the latter.[82] Whether the sustained political mobilisation that resulted from the equally sustained intervention in higher education by reforming governments will increase or diminish the public nature of policy making, appears rather a moot point.[83]

Evaluation

The development of higher education policy as a new sub field of the discipline of government or political science is relatively recent and tends, like the area of policy analysis itself, to be dominated by American models and concepts. This is often helpful inasmuch as it presents a reference point to which studies of particular countries may be anchored. Equally important to bear in mind are the particular circumstances in which the application of this perspective to higher education grew up in the United States. To a large extent, it evolved out of the development of federal aid to higher education and the conditions required by federal authorities for establishments to benefit from that aid. From a European standpoint, the concept of state intervention, as has been intimated earlier, is far from new but a constantly recurring theme. Conversely, the issues posed between institutional liberty, bureaucratic oversight and scholarship are perennial. The legitimacy of state intervention is largely accepted in the European university – though not so readily in the Anglo Saxon world. There is a historical parallel of Mercantilism versus the concept of market forces which is key to understanding much of the difference between American and European universities, and which renders 'collectivist' policies much more legitimate in Scandinavia and continental Europe despite current and passing ideologies. Since the application of American theories and analytic techniques to European circumstances has revealed in these studies the importance of a domain not usually applied to the field of higher education, it is nonetheless relevant to bear in mind some of the differences in value assumptions that underpin them.

Even so, it is undeniable that the inclusion of detailed and informative analyses of the interaction between government and higher education has significantly added to the scope and standing of the Higher Education Research Programme. It has done this in two ways: first, by providing a specifically Swedish contribution to this field at a time when policy studies are in full evolution; second, by providing new insights to the interplay between institutions and actors relatively soon after they have taken place. It is one thing to write the historical record of particular events for the benefit of historians and succeeding generations – an activity in which the Chinese mandarinate of old was indeed adept. But it is no less valuable in furnishing an overview and a perspective for those taking part in the events described.

Policy analysis ought, in the last resort, to prove illuminating to policy-makers, though equally, it ought to be especially careful to avoid establishing a closed dialogue between policy-makers, administrators and those studying them. Failure to bear this in mind could serve to reinforce the tensions between the administrative society and those to whom it ministers. However, the impression is that those in charge of and participating in, the Research programme are very much aware of these dangers. Still, the reverse proposition is also true – namely that the dissemination of studies in a suitable form to others outside the nexus of scholarship and administration has the potential of extending the dialogue even if this is not necessarily of prime concern to scholars in the first instance.

Some of these policy studies have espoused an historical approach inasmuch as they have sought to trace the origins of certain policy issues back over the past forty years. The alliance between policy analysis and the historical approach ought to be fruitful in three ways: first, to understand the thematic issues that, though changing their outward forms as the mode of discours itself alters, nevertheless remain an essential constant. The cultural parameters of policy making as Premfors remarked, are of particular importance and deserve a closer investigation. Second, such an approach may permit the testing of particular theoretical models within the context whose outcome is known, thereby permitting the refinement of such models to a greater degree. Third, the context of contemporary decision-making is, to some extent, the result of options closed off in the past. And to this extent, the historical understanding of the intended or unintended consequences of past planning is no less important than understanding the contemporary side effects of more recent planning. Finally, there are other areas of the Programme that have drawn heavily upon the technique of the historical analogue. The recombination of these studies in the history of public policy within the framework of policy-science ought to be entertained.

Higher education and research policy
(Research about Research)

Following the spread of Humboldt's influence,[84] research and teaching have been the twin pillars of the modern university, although not necessarily within the configuration that Humboldt himself suggested. With the advent of mass higher education, the link between the two has become rather less close in certain countries. In part, this stemmed from the determination of some governments – amongst which are Britain and France – that whilst teaching and research should be funded in some institutions of higher education, others should undertake only the burden of teaching – though subsequent development has often shown this to be a forelorn hope.[85] In part, the weakening of these links is also a result of the current economic crisis. In hard times, money is not available for all teaching institutions to undertake research.[86]

Alongside what might be termed the higher education perspective on research runs another – that of science policy. The origin of this latter which naturally overlaps with higher education, has been traced back to the influence of fundamental scientific research development upon the course of the Second World War. During the post war period in Sweden, no less than in the USA, France and Britain, the machinery for financing and advancing such work was strengthened and expanded.[87] Several factors, particularly during the late Sixties and early Seventies, intervened to bring science policy to the centre of political debate.[88] Prime amongst them was a new interpretation of the role of science policy. In part this stemmed from the recognition that the continual expansion of resources for R&D was no longer possible. Second was the suggestion that science policy itself ought to be redirected towards the qualitative aspects of economic growth, towards a broader concept of welfare and a closer integration of science policy with the totality of social and economic policy.[89]

The linkage between this area and other policy fields – social, economic and environmental – gave rise to the notion of setting up research funding and planning bodies in the main policy areas coming under government responsibility. In Britain, such suggestions formed the bulk of the Rothschild Report's proposals.[90]

Regardless of whether research is looked upon as a crucial element in higher education or whether higher education in turn is seen as a major repository of the nation's capability in R&D, both perspectives raise, once again, the question of the relationship between higher education and government policy though obviously from a different angle to that discussed in the previous section.

In Sweden, the issue of research as a vehicle for national growth and vitality is more a topic of public debate than elsewhere. There are several reasons for this. First, because the role of higher education in the research capacity of the nation is rather larger than in other countries. This derives from Swedish policy that research *should* be concentrated other things being equal inside universities rather than in research institutes outside the higher education system.[91] Second, because Swedish industry tends to be more R&D intensive than its counterparts elsewhere.[92] This gives added weight to the immediacy of science policy research itself. And finally, because research policy assumed all the dimensions of a fully fledged political issue once the debate over the reform of higher education passed into the phase of implementation rather than discussion.[93]

Whereas policy analysis in higher education looked at the interaction between the interests, procedures, mechanisms of policy formulation directed to the issue of higher education reform, the main focus of those dealing with higher education and research policy is upon the utilisation of knowledge, the way it is defined, generated and the use to which it is put through the interplay between higher education research institutes and government based funding bodies. Just as science policy research seeks to analyse those factors and conditions leading to an optimal linkage between research, development and the productive process[94] so research policy studies seek to ascertain those conditions and structures that permit the efficient transfer and utilisation of knowledge from higher education to government or to society represented through the requirements of research funding agencies.

Within the framework of the Programme for Research into Higher Education, there seem to have been two lines of enquiry into research utilisation. The first proceeds from the premisses of the sociology of knowledge and the theory of science, the second from the standpoint of public policy analysis. Whilst the former may be said to be characterised by a 'critical research' perspective, examining in particular the impact of different forms of funding upon the relationship between researchers, practitioners and the generation of different forms of knowledge,[95] the main concern of the latter centred more on the relationship between knowledge utilisation and the public policy making process.[96] Taking a standpoint similar to the Harvard policy analyst, Janet Weiss, Wittrock argued that knowledge utilisation is determined by the structures and characteristics of the relevant policy-making system. Furthermore, in such a system, social research forms only one component amongst myriad different forms of information and beliefs.[97]

Despite different disciplinary perspectives, the outcome of these two approaches may be said to be complementary.[98] Both concluded for instance, in favour of the development of more long term research. Equally, both pointed out the desirability within the Swedish context of less closely directed research although they did so from rather different premisses.

In an examination of the societal utilisation of research, Elzinga held that sectorally driven research not merely posed a fundamental conflict with the norms and procedures of discipline-oriented work, but that it also affected, detrimentally, both the intellectual climate within the research community and its capacity for cognitive reproduction.[99] Elzinga's critique of the sectoral principle rested upon four main arguments: first, that sectoral research represented a departure from the apparant historial autonomy that scientific research once enjoyed. Second, that it led to the bureaucratisation of science – an issue also explored by Premfors in the context of the growing dependence of the state on the purveyors of scientific knowledge.[100] Third, that it tended to politicise the scientific community between those supporters and adversaries of the principle of sectoralisation itself. And finally, that sectoralisation within the field of R&D amounted to all intents and purposes, to the equivalent process of the concentration of capital in industry in the sense that it placed the goals and formulation of policy firmly in the hands of a limited economic and technological elite.[101]

Elzinga's prime concern appeared to lie with the effect of externally driven research upon the cognitive content of research itself and, by extension, its effect on that university community which, historically, had assumed responsibility for the development of many modes of knowledge, alternative as well as dissenting. The university was not just a dépôt of knowledge for industry and government. It was also the means of generating countervailing knowledge traditions which underpinned a crucial notion of cultural and intellectual pluralism to offset the monopolistic control over knowledge content, that sectoralisation seemingly stood for. It was a radical critique which, in many respects, joined that launched by Bergendal vis a vis the effects of the 1977 reform.[102] For Elzinga, 'research on research' seems to pose fundamental issues not merely about the way knowledge and scholarship are developed and controlled but also about the symbolic importance of research as an expression of an unfettered society.

Though many of these values also pervade the work of the Group for the Study of Higher Education and Research Policy, they are less explicitly stated. In the first place, the attitude of the Stockholm group towards the effects of sectoral research is rather more nuanced. Wittrock's study of the Swedish Energy Programme concluded that sectoral science policies did not necessarily undermine either scholarly persuit or the long range mission of higher education.[103] Second, the group's focus lay less upon cognitive development and alternative perspectives to those endorsed by the sectoral principle than upon the way in which research generated knowledge was utilised within the policy-making process. Third, their interest concentrated upon the light such utilisation in a Swedish context could shed upon different theories of planning and implementation.[104] The

Group's investigations fell into two main areas – science policy *stricto sensu*[105] and the utilisation of social science research in policy-making.[106]

In an overview of R&D utilisation in higher education policy, Wittrock and Premfors identified an important change in the models underlying knowledge utilisation in this field. They perceived a decrease in the power of the 'linear engineering model' for explaining policy implementation in higher education, a model which they saw as having accompanied the rise of educational technology during the late Sixties and early Seventies in Sweden.[107] If lack of confidence in the explicative capacity of this model was one reason for its demise, no less important was the development of an option oriented concept of planning. A more detailed investigation of the elements and implications was carried out by Premfors within the context of the interplay between researchers and policy-makers in higher educa-tion.[108]

In this latter exploration which examined R&D from an historical standpoint, Premfors sought to deal with certain 'interactive' issues: to what extent were R&D activities in the social science field subsequently utilised in policy-making? What characteristics of the policy-making process influenced the extent to which such knowledge was used? What were the dominant ideas in Swedish research policy regarding research utilisation? His conclusions were unequivocal. In Sweden, the role of research in higher education policy making was, he suggested, marginal. In his study, which covered the period from 1935 onward, he observed no instance of policy change where research made the crucial difference.[109] Nor was the partisan use of research decisive in influencing policy change. And, finally, those areas where social science research was held to be authoritative involved only minor issues of policy or took the form of fact-gathering exercise.[110] Here was evidence of the inappropriateness of the 'linear, engineering model' as a means of understanding the interplay between research and policy-making in the social sciences. *Faute de mieux*, one had to conclude that though such research *did* have an impact, and an important one, its function was to *enlighten* policy-makers and in a way best described as diffuse rather than specific. In short, research raises the level of debate in unpredictable ways.

The question which arises from this, and which is being currently addressed by the Group for the Study of Higher Education at Stockholm, is how far these findings may be applicable to realms other than Higher Education or to research in areas other than the social sciences? The current project, empirically based, concentrates on the relationship between sectoral commissioning bodies and their potential customers. Its purpose is two-fold: first, to trace and describe those obstacles to the interchange between cognitive production and the policy-making process; second, to test within the Swedish context, certain hypotheses developed in the United States about the concomitants of efficient R&D usage.[111]

58

Evaluation

The area of higher education and research policy stands at the intersection of several established disciplinary fields and sub-fields: sociology, history of ideas, theory of science, sociology of knowledge and policy analysis. Some might suggest that this 'problem area' of the Research on higher education programme is *more* related to the current concerns of central government administration than others. This would imply wrongly that other areas, previously analysed, are *less* obviously related to current government concerns. But it is nevertheless the case that, by the very nature of this research, it is addressed in prime instance, to government. If 'learning about learning' is addressed to academics, teachers and students, 'Research about research' would seem to be addressed to scholars, researchers and decision-makers. If the former holds up Caliban's mirror to the grass roots of the ascending hierarchy, the latter presents it with no less firmness to the top of the descending hierarchy.

Though such symmetry may be entirely coincidental, the incorporation of Research policy into the Research on Higher Education Programme has provided an additional dimension not often found within the field of higher education studies. This is not to say that research policy studies are absent in other countries, but they tend to be less aligned with the study of higher education than for example with the academic study of government or economics. The presence of Research Policy in the higher education research programme has contributed to – as well as being at the same time, a manifestation of the shift from – quantitative, empirical research of a conjunctural nature towards the qualitative, theoretical and longer-term perspective.

Higher education and research policy is an area where Swedish contacts with international scholarship in the United States, Britain and West Germany have been particularly fruitful and of a sustained nature. This is reflected in the high degree of publications in international journals as well as close collaboration with scholars working on similar projects in different countries. One thinks in this connexion of the work currently being undertaken into similar domains in Brunel University, London and the close ties that exist between the Group for the Study of higher education and research policy and the Group for the study of comparative higher education at University of California, Los Angeles. Other ties exist between the PAREX research consortium in West Germany and the Göteborg group. It is not easy to ascertain, other than on the basis of personal insight and intuition, either the intensity or the quality of these exchanges. But there is enough internal evidence in documents put out by both groups and on the basis of personal interviews, to suggest that the speed at which ideas are exchanged and built into research proposals and suggestions for future research, is indeed very great.

Some years ago, suggestions were made within that part of the Swedish scholarly community working on 'research about research' that there was a signal absence of work corresponding to the 'American style' of the sociology of science or to the 'British style' social studies of science.[112] This may be correct when taken within the framework of those disciplinary sub-fields. It is, equally the case that, if one alters the perspective to that of studies on higher education, there is every indication that Swedish work on science policy research techniques stands as a very real contribution that field as well as to broadening the general perspective on higher education itself. Here it must be said that not only does Swedish research appear – like Uriah the Hittite – to be 'in the forefront of the battle'. But it is also redefining the boundaries wherein that battle shall be fought.

There are two other considerations that give support to this judgement. Sectoralisation of research, the advent of greater government regulation in the affairs of higher education, concern about the country's research capacity are not just Swedish developments. They are to be found elsewhere in Western Europe. That such issues emerged earlier in Sweden and have attracted researchers into examining them could well mean that such research is itself in advance of similar projects also launched in the light of these preoccupations elsewhere. Seen from this angle, it may well be that research into this area of higher education's difficulties will become a major issue elsewhere as the problems already anticipated in Sweden assume greater acuity in other places. If this is the case, then current Swedish research on research policy within the framework of higher education represents the shape of things to come and, like the industrial development of Wilhelmine Germany compared to that of Victorian Britain, research here will have jumped over a stage that others have had to work their way through.

5

Assessment and evaluation

A few honest men are better than numbers.

Oliver Cromwell to the Rump Parliament, September 1643.

Introduction

In this part of our report, we turn our attention away from the detail of the research undertaken by the Programme and seek instead to examine its status as a vehicle for scholarly enterprise and as a scholarly community. We will then go on to try and place the Programme in an international context by comparing it with its counterparts elsewhere – mainly in Britain and France. Perhaps failure to take the United States into account is an omission. Whilst not denying this, there are reasons for so doing. First, there is a difference of scale both as regards men, money and resources. The higher education research community is so vast in the United States that it probably represents more than the total number of scholars active in this field throughout Western Europe. Second, it is interesting to look at the development of higher education studies in Western European countries where the state of the art and the history of the University may be presumed to be comparable.

A consolidated community?
Views of scholars on the development of the
Research on higher education programme

In view of earlier evaluations of the various areas of research contained in the Research into higher education programme, there can be little doubt as to the success of that community in terms of its vitality, its scholarly output or the introduction of new and theoretical perspectives to the field of Higher Education. Amongst those whom we interviewed, there was wide agreement about the indispensable part of the Programme in facilitating and encouraging the development of those perspectives. Though we would not go as far as the young researcher who argued that, for decades no theoretical research had been possible under the sponsorship of other funding agencies, we would nevertheless endorse his enthusiasm in defending the contribution to scholarship of the NBUC Programme.

But a Community is not just the presence of scholars working in isolation on related topics. It is also the exchange of ideas and the cross fertilisation of interest that one discipline may provide those working in another. We have already touched upon the role of the continuing series of conferences, seminars and 'problem area' discussions that, sponsored by the NBUC, continue to nourish this exchange. This institutionalised interplay between centre and periphery, between R&D policy makers, decision-makers and researchers is one of the strengths of the Programme. Equally important, however, are the cross institutional links between researchers working on the same problem area or using the same methodology to explore differing areas of interest. The development of what might be called a second level network, bringing together scholars on a sustained basis outside official occasions is especially important in an area relatively new and where the overall size of the scholarly community is relatively small.

But these outstanding features cannot obviate the fact that, by its nature, the study of Higher Education is a fragile field. Its fragility – as also its strength – rests upon the fact that it is an interdisciplinary area which is subject to both centrefugal and centrepetal forces. Put another way, it depends on whether individual scholars in it see Higher Education as a vehicle for forwarding work in what they consider to be their principal discipline or whether, on the contrary, they are interested in pursuing the applications of a particular theory across different areas, one of which happens to be Higher Education. Those who see Higher Education in the former light may be said to constitute the centrepetal forces and those conversely, of the latter persuasion, the centrefugal.

In an effort to see how far these influences were at play inside the Research programme, we asked interviewees what they would be doing if they were not funded by the National Board of Universities and Colleges. Like most leading questions, it had several objectives; in part, it was designed to see whether they would have envisaged similar subjects for research only funded from different sources; in part to see what other academic or disciplinary areas would have attracted their interest. Typical of the centrepetal tensions inside the Programme was the reply given by one researcher working in the social sciences area:

> 'For me, the problems are of a general kind. It isn't important if they are related to *higher* education or if it's related to *lower* educational levels. I see them more as examples of the more general and theoretical topics which I am interested in working on. If I didn't get money from research into higher education, then surely, I would get money for projects at other levels . . . There are more general and theoretical and methodological problems elsewhere.'

An analysis of similar replies revealed that they tended to be made by people with relatively long term involvement in the Programme and they also tended to be people with a sense of a strong disciplinary identity. If Higher Education is an area to which they apply the theories and techniques developed within that context, their frame of reference appears, intellectually at least, to remain outside it. Such references to an external disciplinary frame are important from a number of points of view. First, they show once again the power of what we have called earlier 'the disciplinary cultures'. Second, they show the genesis of potential difficulties that are also to be found in sectoral research in other countries between the internalist values of academia and the problem centred concerns of administration.[1]

The latter is an especially important point since it shows the likely outcome in moving the Research programme itself over to long-term work and also the justifications of so doing. In Higher Education Policy and Administration for example, there is a dynamic in the intellectual development and interests of 'discipline oriented' scholars that the Research programme has both harnessed and forwarded. The development of general administrative theory and the emergence of substantive areas of factual data which may be applied to other contexts, is a testimony to the intellectual opportunities the Programme permits its Political Science participants. But it also strengthens the 'internalist values' of this particular section of the higher education research community. Having developed such interests it is, in a curious manner, no longer so closely tied to the programme. Seen from this angle, one might argue that from the standpoint of 'discipline' oriented scholars, higher education is a passing phase of development, one in which theories brought from elsewhere may be further tested in a different context and refined still further. Once refined, they may be re-applied to more traditional disciplinary areas.

This process may be seen as evidence of the fragility of the Programme. It can also be argued that Higher Education is an area which lends itself to an interdisciplinary approach. We agree but with the proviso that if the 'interdisciplinary approach' is worthwhile maintaining, it requires from time to time that those involved in it go back to their original fields to draw further strength within a 'disciplinary perspective' later to contribute to the 'interdisciplinary perspective'. Established academics seem very attuned to this need.

If these are some of the tensions resulting from the centrepetal forces inside the programme what of the centrefugal? These are most evident amongst younger scholars whose early work was undertaken within the framework of the Programme and who tend, on balance, to more 'issue oriented' than discipline oriented. The position of the 'issue oriented' community was summed up for us as follows:

> 'Were it not for these specific ear-marked funds, there would be very few people working in this area. If you look at the amount of higher education research that is financed out of other sources, it's very little and it would be very little. I am completely sure that I wouldn't be in higher education . . . One could of course easily imagine a situation when some people who have been productive in this area turn elsewhere or whose interests become more peripheral to higher education. Whether it would be possible to have a new set of recruits . . . is difficult to tell.'

For this group within the higher education community, scholarly maturity does not necessarily impel them back into their fundamental discipline since that is not their basic reference point. Rather, it leads to their moving into other issue areas where, once again, the techniques and insights developed within the context of higher education research may be applied. Arguably, the process involved is similar to that found amongst the 'discipline oriented' insofar as it involves higher education as transitionary phase in their intellectual interests. The difference is, however, the direction they take which is not towards a reinforcement of a disciplinary perspective so much as the continuation of applying an 'interdisciplinary perspective' to other fields.

In both cases, it will be a most delicate task for those guiding the higher education research programme to accord the concerns of government to the dynamic of scholarship amongst those whom it has sponsored in the past. There is, however, a rather different standpoint from which one may view such developments. This is to see such acquisition of knowledge in the area of higher education as constituting a stock of intellectual knowledge and manpower which, whilst it may not have to be called upon immediately, may be so in the future. There is no reason why those who have worked in the field in the past should not do so in the future. And, indeed, it is arguable that to call later upon scholars whose work in the meantime has benefitted from experience acquired in other areas, is to have the additional benefit of that experience. What is highly important, however, is to ensure sufficient numbers in the 'pool' that would allow such a policy.

Some concern about the relative financial fragility of the Programme emerged in the course of our talks. This can be viewed from a number of different angles – either as a matter of institutional continuity, job security or career structure. To some extent, these are interrelated:

> 'When you work in sector research in Sweden, you are not very socially secure (sic). Myself, I know I have work for X years. But how long can you accept these terms? You can say to yourself, "It's going to work". And perhaps it will . . . but all the time, you are getting older . . . It's really to do with jobs.'

Such off-the-cuff remarks should not be dismissed because they may reflect the personal anguish of a particular individual. Rather, they raise some fundamental problems about the nature of research work in general at a time when promotions are blocked and research, as the Swedish government has itself noted, is becoming the domain of an ageing profession.[2]

This latter aspect is not, however, unique to the Research on Higher Education Programme but appears to be generic to Swedish research in general. Whether this is the result of reluctance by students to continue with a long initiation into research training or whether it reflects a certain decision not to seek to identify some who might so be induced for fear of discriminating against the majority who may not, is a moot point. One should note, en passant, that the problem of obtaining sufficient numbers of students to ensure the country's future research capacity in ten years time is an issue not confined to Sweden. It may also be seen in West Germany,[3] Norway,[4] France,[5] and, of course, the United Kingdom.

Job security and career structure are, of course, related to wider issues in Swedish academia. But they assume a particularly acute form when applied in the context of higher education research. This is for several reasons: first, because as we have pointed out, this field is more prone to internal pressures which, if not underwritten by a more substantial funding and institutional base, might lead to its dispersal into other areas; second, because the career structure of those involved in full-time higher education research within the Programme is not related to the field of higher education so much as to the disciplinary areas, departments and organisations in which they are at present located. This may not be a problem for established scholars with guaranteed posts. But it would seem to pose considerable difficulties for younger members of the community who have yet to attain that status. Moreover, this factor may well serve to accentuate the pull from other areas of study with better chances of advancement. Third, because in the last resort, stability in that community depends strictly on maintaining higher education as an issue with a high political profile or, put another way, that it figure high on the governments' current agenda. Issue oriented research is, of course, always subject to this latter constraint. But since so great a part of the research commissioned in the area of higher education is of this nature, this consideration looms larger in the consciousness of that community.

The fundamental question that arises out of this is: how to preserve the knowledge, skills and expertise which the Programme has nurtured? A number of suggestions were broached in the course of many interviews and or discussions. One proposal was that there should be a species of contingency research fund attached to particular departments. Another suggested limited but sustained support for a small number of research units which, by competing with each other would ensure the maintenance of quality. This, it was pointed out, might be a useful means of anchoring staff to the field of higher education. A third variant was for a kind of 'think tank'. It would have a dual mission – on the one hand to engage in research feeding into decision-making a central government level and, on the other, to conduct 'alternative research', independent of the signals coming from government. There is much to be said for the latter, more especially since the exploration of issues outside the immediate concern of government sponsored research appears to be an area that many in the higher education community consider to be of increasing importance. However, an institute of this form may pose certain difficulties insofar as it could represent a violation of the principle underwriting much of Swedish research that it should be located in the university.

A further possibility would be to develop an institute for the study of comparative higher education policy as a sub section of the Institute for International Education and to affect some of the resources here to this end. Since the National Board of Education is also engaged in bolstering long range research in the schools section the intellectual cross cutting that might result, despite differences in the policies of research steering, might well prove beneficial.

To the question 'Is the higher education research community in Sweden a consolidated community?' our answer is unequivocally, 'Yes'. But it stands at a particular point in its development where maturing scholarly interests could bring about its dispersal. Rethinking research priorities in the light of evolving scholarly and government concern and interests is a necessary but not sufficient measure on its own to meet this potential outcome of dispersal. It may well be that, as sectorial agencies assume responsibility for long term research, more opportunities may impart a greater degree of stability in the research community. But in the long run, the issue is more basic.

In essence, the underlying question, best tackled sooner rather than later, is what place ought higher education to have in the broader scholarly community from the standpoint of career structures and reasonable allocation of posts?

Higher education in Britain and France: the organisation of two research communities

So far our evaluation of the Research on higher education programme has been in terms of its chronological development, its changing research perspectives and its internal, intellectual unfolding. In short, we have compared it to itself in the Swedish academic context. But how does it compare from the standpoint of its organisation, its relationship with government and its intellectual interests with its Western European counterparts as Britain and France?

Britain

Some eight years ago, one commentator noted that "it would be misleading to imply that there is *any organisation* (our italics) for higher education R&D in the United Kingdom. There are a number of individuals and agencies concerned with various aspects of this topic but they are in no way coordinated with one another.[7]

Broadly speaking, the picture holds good today. As in Sweden, the main impetus for the development of this field of research was provided by government in the form of the Higher Education Research Unit, set up as the main research arm to the Robbins Committee and disbanded in 1973. What impetus still comes from central government is not applied to the general sponsorship of higher education research *per se* so much as to notable individuals within it. Thus the essential characteristic of this community in Britain is its diasporic nature. In part, this may be attributed to two factors not present in Sweden to the same degree. The first would appear to be the relative lack of access to government. Research undertaken tends to be destined for those within the higher education community rather than to inform government decision making. Nor is the academic research community invited to provide officially blessed external evaluations of government work.[8] The second factor is the considerable importance of research funding from private sources and foundations – especially the Nuffield, Rowntree and the Leverhulme foundations. This latter has recently financed a series of seminars on the future of higher education in Britain. Important though these seminars have been in giving a focus to the higher education community in Britain, they appear to underline what might be termed the 'private nature' and the degree of self-organisation that characterises this body in the United Kingdom.

Thus by contrast to the Research into higher education programme, British research in higher education is not, officially at least, linked directly with policy-making, though there are suggestions that it ought to be. There has always been some concern about the lack of a formal locus for that community which has official sanction and long term backing. From 1976 onwards, and particularly following the debate on the Leverhulme sponsored seminars, various proposals have been aired. Some have suggested a National Institute of Education, others have come up with the notion of a 'counter ministry' to provide analyses from an independent viewpoint to the Department of Education and Science, local education authorities or to relevant Parliamentary sub committees.[9]

In the absence of such an institute, the Society for the Research into Higher Education acts to some extent, as a focal point for some of the higher education community in Britain. Founded in 1964, it is organised both nationally and locally, holds an annual conference and various meeting throughout the year at regional level. A largely self-sustaining body, it publishes Research Abstracts, a Journal, *Studies in higher education* and has a current membership of around 600.

It would be difficult to categorise this community other than on an intuitive basis, but one has the impression that, overall, it tends to be less research-based and, compared with its Swedish counterpart, more concerned with matters of a didactical nature – teaching techniques, staff development being major areas of interest especially after the Society for Research into Higher Education added development as an area of interest in the early Seventies. *Grosso modo*, it is probably correct, on balance, to see three levels within the higher education community in Britain. The first consists of those interested in didactical and organisational issues but not active in researching them on a sustained and systematic basis. The second consists of those members, usually drawn from Departments of Education in either the public or the university sector, primarily concerned with the organisation, administration and didactical elements of staff training, academic development programmes and the research concerns of ex teacher training establishments as an outgrowth. The third group, which has a high international profile, is mainly research oriented, dealing with such aspects as the economics of education, issues of *systemic* administration, organisation and finance, policy analysis. The fact that this British community appears to consist of scattered and divers interests, relies considerably on private sources for funding, and involves areas that in Sweden have been split off from the Research on higher education programme – for instance, staff development means that the development of cohesive and coordinated research is virtually excluded by the nature of higher education community itself. There are, rather, a series of different communities which, like the oecumenical movement within the Churches, occasionally come together in a spirit of good-will and understanding without necessarily adopting the other's theology or liturgy!

France
If the focus of the British higher education research community tends to be less strong than some of its members would desire and to lie in the main, outside government, the position of its French counterpart is, if anything, rather more nebulous. Certainly, there is a strong funding frame imposed by central government and all the stronger for there being a virtual absence of substanital private funding sources. Since May 1981, with the disbandment of the Ministry of Higher Education, higher education research – such as it is – has found itself divided between the formal legal oversight of the National Ministry of Education and the Ministry for Technology and Industry under whose ambit the main research organising body, the *Centre National de la Recherche Scientifique* is now located.[10]

This reorganisation has led to some dispute as to whether educational research in general and higher education by extension, ought not to be brought firmly under the aegis of the Ministry of Technology and Industry as a means of linking the imperatives of science policy to the necessary reforms that would have to take place in education to meet them. At the moment, the question is still unresolved.

The *Centre National de la Recherche Scientifique* is the main fund providing source and is responsible for fundamental research in 41 disciplines grouped into eight sectors. Over the years, the influence of this body on the structure and organisation of French research has been paramount. Based on a research organisation which, itself is said to be founded upon a physical science model, research groups are organised into teams, some located as independent units *inside* the CNRS, others – known as associated units are located inside higher education establishments and a third category – known as 'independent units' exist outside higher education completely. In contrast to Sweden, it is not expected that the universities shall be responsible for the major part of the country's fundamental research. Much of it, as has been intimated, is carried on either inside CNRS internal units or in groups external to higher education. And, in contrast to Britain, there exists a separate corps of full-time research staff on long-term funding with tenured status outside the university.

There is no research programme which is exclusively devoted to higher education research on its own. Research in this area is rather, undertaken within the general framework of institutes whose main interests lie in the area of the economics of education and the linkage between education and the labour market through research into the demand for and the supply of different types of educational and professional qualifications, the *Centre de Recherche pour l'Etude et l'Observation des Conditions de Vie* (CREDOC) with interests centred on research into consumer behaviour (and higher education from this particular angle) which is based in Paris and the *Institut de Recherche sur l'Economie de l'Education* (IREDU) at the University of Dijon. With the context of these institutes, which are financed by the CNRS, higher education figures as an ancilliary area, tied to the substantive disciplinary commitment of the particular institute. Amongst others whose work has at various times taken them into higher education, are the *Centre d'Etudes Sociologiques* and the *Centre de Sociologie des Organisations*, the former being involved with the sociology of knowledge approaches and the latter, inter alia, with issues of systems theory, decision-making and systems organisation. Thus, though the contribution to theoretical work in France might be both original and of high scholarly quality, higher education as a field on its own or as a conscious community standing in its own right, has yet to emerge. As yet it is subject to institutional fragmentation and specialisation, features that are accentuated by the substantial division – though by no means totally impermeable – that exists between France's university teachers on the one hand and its tenured researchers on the other.

We noted in the British context that a considerable amount of interest and research is devoted to didactical aspects within the higher education community. Our impression is that this forms a relatively minor concern in France. Furthermore, there are constraints upon undertaking research not directly related to teaching courses in French universities. Machin, in his examination of the social science research system in France, attributes this to policies of successive governments which resulted in teachers having to work longer hours, but leaves them with neither time nor incentive for research other than in their main teaching discipline.[11]

However, one major vehicle for the study of higher education in France are the various expert commissions set up on an *ad hoc* basis to deal with specific issues and to come up with proposals for their solution. Amongst these one may cite the Massenet Report on research careers[12] and the more recent study on the financing of universities undertaken by the Freville Commission.[13] But these though they might contribute to public discussion, influence government thinking or improve knowledge about key issues in higher education, are independent of a research community *en tant que telle* in higher education.

In short, the heavily sectoralised structure of the French research community, its distribution amongst institutes with a specific disciplinary basis and the relatively tenuous links with the teaching sector of higher education, have militated against the emergence of Higher Education as an identifiable and coherent intellectual community in France. A final factor, though its influence is difficult to assess, is the considerable amount of middle-level in-house research that is carried out within the National Ministry of Education, particularly into such matters as student flows through the education system. This, allied to the system of 'contracting out' research to specialised institutes, means that the need to develop such a community is seen to be neither pressing nor necessary by many officials. Thus, in contrast to Sweden, there is in France neither the will at the top nor, in contrast to Britain, is there the energy at the grass roots to bring about a recognisable, self-standing community of researchers specialising in contemporary issues of Higher Education as a main area of scholarly enquiry.

6 A conclusion, a criticism and some suggestions

> There is a method which ... is not characteristic of philosophy alone; it is, rather, the one method of all *rational discussion*, and therefore of the natural sciences as well as of philosophy. The method I have in mind is that of stating one's problem clearly and of examining its various proposals *critically*.
>
> **Karl Popper**, *The Logic of Scientific Discoveries*, London, 1959. p. 16.

Introduction

In this report, we have set out to examine and evaluate higher education research in Sweden. We have done this from a number of perspectives which may be said to represent three main approaches, the historical, the comparative and the international. In Chapter Two of this report, we sought to locate higher education research in the broader, political and cultural values of Swedish society as *we perceived them*. This is important since without an explicit statement of what we understood by these values, it would have been difficult to grasp the wider societal context in which the Research into higher education programme is located. It would have been far less easy to grasp the particular significance of the changes in the internal disciplinary perspective of the Programme which was reflected in the inclusion after 1976 of what we have termed the 'value disciplines' – history

72

and philosophy *inter alia*. Subsequently in Chapter Three, we examined the historical development of the Programme, its funding priorities, procedures for treating applications, its system of 'interactive steering' and its method of 'dialoguing' between interested parties. In Chapter Four, the main part of the report, we analysed a selection of projects representing the main aspects developed in the Programme and sought to evaluate each section in function to its contribution to scholarship and its location within, as well as those influences deriving from, the international community of scholars. Finally, in Chapter Five, we compared the place of the higher education research community in Sweden to its counterparts in two other countries – Britain and France.

The Swedish higher education research community

In Sweden as in other countries, research into higher education has developed as a separate field only recently. What, however, characterises the Swedish edition of this domain is its coherence, its solid research base and, above all, its very rapid development. It is evident, for instance, that compared with Britain, research on Higher Education in Sweden is more closely related to government policy-making and is regarded as a valuable contribution to this. Compared with France, where the concept of higher education research as a self-standing area is largely absent, this area in Sweden is clearly identifiable and constitutes an active corpus of knowledge. One has the impression that one of the most valuable aspects of official sponsorship for this programme has been the speed at which additional perspectives have been brought into this area of study. One thinks, by comparison of the way in which the theory of science, public administration or policy analysis – which, though present in Britain higher education research – fail to loom so large or to have assumed to important a place as is the case in Sweden. In Britain, it appears as if studies within these disciplines stand as pioneering undertakings rather than being seen as one of the usual tools and intellectual perspectives that figure in higher education as a matter of course. The same observation can be made with reference to the comparative approach to higher education whether from a perspective of institutional development, systemic evolution or its place in the policy. It is significant, however, that this approach, developed mainly in the United States, has rapidly been introduced by younger scholars closely in touch with current American work in this field. As yet, neither the British, still less the French, studies in higher education have shown substantial interest in this aspect of contemporary development. It is, however, only right to point out that such an approach is fully integrated into the more *historically-based* studies of higher education, particularly those dealing with the early modern period of Western European history.

A criticism of the programme

If we have a criticism of the way higher education research has developed in Sweden, we would say that it tends to concentrate over much on what might be called 'Official Sweden' – the Sweden where reforms are discussed, explored, weighed and implemented. As one of our interviewees reminded us, this is but one side of the picture:

> 'There are people in the civil service and people in the university world. They live in a different world from other people. They live in a world where you do reforms in society. There are two societies in Sweden. The one is the reforming niveau and the other is the real world. You will find very few mechanisms to see the consequences of reforms in the real world. You have a public life of reforms in Sweden and a private life in which people are very little interested.'

Recent discussion, in Sweden has suggested that this gulf is, if anything, becoming wider.[1]

This is not sufficient reason on its own to cause us to suggest that more attention ought to be paid to developments in such areas that might reflect this growing gulf inside higher education – for example, quality of student life and aspirations – still less to suggest that more interest be taken in such matters as the cultures of the various communities, teachers as well as administrators, that have part of their being in higher education. Yet, when taken in conjunction with research that is already involved on the fringes of such matters – for instance; studies on professional cultures noted in chapter four, pp 38–43; the initial explorations of the views and attitudes of academics, pp 44–48; and the whole issue that subtends the last two sections, pp 49–58, namely the problem of implementation – there is sufficient indication within the programme to press for further development of these analyses along such lines.[2]

Suggestions for future research

There has been some discussion within the Group for the Study of Higher Education and Research Policy about the possibility of introducing such fields as anthropology or to undertake such enquiries from a 'cultural perspective'. There are two possible objections to this suggestion. First, the incorporation of a further discipline into the Programme will require an expansion in its funding if it is to avoid the situation of 'robbing Peter to pay Paul'. In other words, if additional disciplinary coverage is to be provided perhaps, it ought not to be at the expense of those areas of strength already developed and flourishing. The reason for this remark is linked to the stage of intellectual development in the programme as a whole which, as we noted earlier (pp 62–67) is already subject to internal pressures. These ought not to be exacerbated. Second is the question of the so-called 'cultural perspective'. This is generally understood as a series of qualitatively oriented micro level studies in the areas we have already noted. But the 'cultural perspective' is just that – it is a perspective that is subject to wide variation depending on the particular discipline – history, sociology, public administration or political science – alternatively, problem approach – policy analysis, phenomenography, the history of ideas – within which it is located. It is not a self-standing field. For this reason, if a 'cultural perspective' is worth taking on board, it would best be as part of a substantive project allocated to such fields. If, as has been argued, the cultural standpoint may furnish valuable insights into the heart of higher education's 'private lives', then it is worth developing it as a sub-section for *all* relevant projects across the disciplinary areas. Another possibility is to hold the particular research area constant – for instance, student sub cultures – and have different 'cultural approaches from within the relevant disciplines analyse it each from their particular interpretation.

There are, we would suggest, advantages to be gained from this way of proceding. First, it would permit the introduction of the 'cultural perspective' without necessarily involving the need for additional expenditure since such a perspective would be encouraged within already existing teams and resources. Second, it would allow the further development of a cross disciplinary dimension without many of the weaknesses inherant in too sustained a commitment to 'interdisciplinarity' which, as we have pointed out earlier[3] is ephemeral. Third such a *modus operandi* would, in all likelihood, afford further opportunities for cross institutional collaboration, thereby reinforcing an already notable feature of the Programme as a whole. And, finally, it may serve to dampen down those centrepetal and centrefugal forces within the programme through underpinning the notion of a common enterprise which, hopefully, might stabilise scholars' commitment to it.

At various points in our analysis of the projects, we noted the importance of the use of either historical techniques or the espousal or what we termed the 'historical analogue' to clarify certain contemporary issues in Higher Education such as disciplinary and professional ethics, the rise of certain professions etc. We suggested in this connexion, that the recombination of 'implementation studies' with this approach through the examination of past issues the outcome of which is known, would prove a useful vehicle to refine general theory and also to seek possible counter examples in the Swedish context, that might permit its revision or elaboration.

There may be new insights to be had by applying the purely historical approach to the area of public policy – an area which, if our impressions are correct, is not overdeveloped in Sweden. However, if history is not to act as a further reinforcement to what we have termed the study of 'official Sweden' (though this may equally be seen as a *legitimate* area of interest) some attention ought to be paid to examining the impact of national policies upon the local level, be it institutional or societal, in short upon 'hidden Sweden'.

A number of possible topics spring to mind, though they are presented here simply *à titre d'exemple*. Amongst them ought to be the role of local interest groups upon national policy making in higher education both from a contemporary and from an historical perspective; the concomitants of public participation in higher education other than as students, the changing image of the university as perceived by the local community and its representatives; the way in which the university is regarded as contributing to the quality of life in the local community; the impact of a national elite upon local community level – the development of the academic community as part of the community.

Some might argue that these are merely 'highfalutin' terms for the old issue of 'town and gown relations'. And it may well be that the acrimony, jealousy and mutual disrespect that characterised such relations in many West European sub-cultures from the time of François Villon onwards,[4] exist to a lesser degree in Sweden. Were this the case, it would be important to know why Sweden is so exceptional.

Studies such as these would constitute a second 'qualitative jump' within the Research on Higher Education Programme, since, in essence, they move beyond the issue of implementation to that of the 'impact' of reform. They also relocate the focus of interest upon the interplay not between government and higher education, but between higher education and the local community in which it is situated. It would seem to us that this is a logical and desirable next step especially in view of the 1977 reform and the recent changes in the governance structure of the Swedish comprehensive university.

A final caveat from outside

However, one should be aware of the implications of such studies seen from the standpoint of one of those salient values that have hitherto characterised both Swedish society and higher education research. One of these, we noted, was the concept of *Enhetlighet*. The concept of territorial unity and equal provision runs throughout the Research into Higher Education Programme and is symbolically represented by the fact that by far the greater part of its undertakings has underpinned a view that is national and operationalised at the *macro* level. In proposing that more attention be paid to the micro level or to the local level, one should perhaps be aware of the implications such an approach holds for one of the essential and outstanding features of Swedish national culture.

Notes

Chapter 1

1 For the various perspectives see Burton R. Clark, *Perspectives on higher education: eight disciplinary and comparative views*, Berkeley, 1983, University of California Press.

2 Guy Neave, *Equality, ideology and educational policy: an essay in the history of ideas*, Amsterdam, 1977, Institut d'Education de la Fondation Européenne de la Culture. pp.1–2.

3 Fritz Ringer, *The Rise of the German mandarins: the German academic profession 1890–1932*, Cambridge (Mass) 1969, Belknapp Press.

4 Guy Neave, *Patterns of Equality: the influence of new structures in European higher education upon equality of opportunity*, Windsor (England) 1976, National Foundation for Educational Research.

5 Pierre Bourdieu & Jean-Claude Passeron, *Les Heritiers*, Paris, 1969, Editions de Minuit.

6 A. Gouldner, *The future of the intellectuals and the rise of the new class*, New York, 1979, Seabury Press.

Chapter 2

1 Margaret Scotford Archer, 'The sociology of education systems', *address to the International Sociological Association*, Paris August 1980, (mimeo)

2 Urban Dahllöf, *Reforming higher education and external studies in Sweden and Australia*, Uppsala, 1977, Uppsala Studies in Education, No. 3.

3 Guy Neave, 'La notion de limites comme modèle des liens existant entre l'Université et l'Etat', *CRE Information*, No. 58, 1982

4 Jan-Erik Lane, *Higher education in a Scandinavian comparative perspective*, Umeå 1981, Statsvetenskapliga institutionen Forskningsrapport 1981:15, p.13

5 Bengt Gesser, 'Students: education and politics' (English translation) *Forskning om Utbildning* no. 2, 1978.

6 Tore Frängsmyr, 'The Enlightenment in Sweden' in Roy Porter & Mkulas Teich, (eds) *The Enlightenment in national context*, Cambridge, 1977, University Press pp. 168–172.

7 Lennart Svensson, 'The state and higher education: a sociological critique from Sweden', *European Journal of Education*, vol. 17, No. 3, 1982, pp. 297–303.

8 for this see Karl-Heinz Gruber, 'Higher education and the state in Austria: an historical and institutional approach', *European journal of Education, op. cit.*

9 Guy Neave, 'The Regional dimension: some considerations from a European perspective', in Michael Shattock (ed), *Structure and Governance of higher education*, Guildford (England), 1983, Society for Research into Higher Education.

10 *Programme of the Swedish Social Democratic Party adopted by the 1975 party congress*, Borås, 1975, Sjuhäradsbygdens Tryckeri, p. 10.

11 *ibid.*, p. 11.

12 Lars Engqvist, 'A Personal view', *The Swedish Labour Movement*, Stockholm, 1982, A-Pressen AB, p. 17.

13 Folkpartiet, *Engelsk version av Folkpartiet*, 1982/3 (mimeo).

14 Jörgen Westerståhl, 'From belief in authority to individualism', (English translation) *Dagens Nyheter*, October 15th 1982.

15 Tage Erlander, 'A Personal view', *The Swedish Labour Movement, op. cit.*, p. 9.

16 Donald Hancock, 'The Swedish welfare state: prospects and contradictions', *The Wilson Quarterly*, vol. 1, No. 3 (Fall) 1977.

17 Rowland Eustace, 'British higher education and the state', *European Journal of Education, op. cit.*, pp. 283ff.

18 Birgitta Odén. Interview, Lund, November 24th 1982.

19 Kjell Härnqvist & Jarl Bengtsson, *Educational reform and educational equality*, Göteborg, 1973, Department of Education. Arnold J. Heidenheimer, 'The politics of educational reform: explaining the different outcomes of school comprehensivisation in Sweden and West Germany', *Comparative Education Review*, vol. 18, 1974
Leon Boucher, *The Swedish tradition in Education*, Oxford, 1982, Pergamon Press.
Torsten Husén, *Talent, Meritocracy, Equality*, Amsterdam, 1974, Martinus Nijhoff.

20 Rune Premfors, *Integrated higher education: the Swedish experience*, Stockholm, 1981, Department of Political Science, p. 6.

21 *ibid.*, p. 29.

22 Husén, *op. cit.*

23 Neave, *Equality, ideology and educational policy . . . op. cit.*

24 Guy Neave, *How They Fared: the impact of the comprehensive school upon the university*, London, 1975, Routledge & Kegan Paul.

25 Mr. Hans Löwbeer. Interview, Stockholm, November 19th 1982.

26 Inga Elgqvist Saltzman & Susan Opper, *Equality and internationalism: two concepts at the forefront of educational transformation in Sweden?*, Uppsala, 1981, Uppsala Reports on Education, No. 12, p. 35.

27 Löwbeer interview occ. cit.

28 Thomas Anton, 'Policy-making and political culture in Sweden', *Scandinavian Political Studies*, No. 4, 1969.

29 Guy Neave, 'R&D for education: Britain compared to Sweden', *Political Quarterly*, vol. 44, No. 3, 1973.

30 Olof Ruin. Interview, Stockholm, November 12th 1982.

31 Richard Scase, *Readings in the Swedish class structure*, Oxford, 1976, Pergamon Press pp. 4–5.

32 *ibid.*, p. 5.

33 John Plamenatz, *Man and Society*, vol. II, London, 1963, Longmans, p. 457

34 L.J. Sharp, 'The social scientist and policy-making in Britain and America', in Martin Bulmer (ed), *Social Policy Research*, London 1978, Macmillan, p. 69.

35 Carol H. Weiss, 'The many meanings of research utilisation', *Public Administration Review*, September/October 1979.

36 Gunnar Bergendal (ed), *Knowledge and Higher Education*, Stockholm, 1983, Almqvist & Wiksell International.

37 Scase, *op. cit.*, p. 4.

38 Ingemar Nilsson, *The Art of Medicine and Medical Science*, Göteborg, 1982 Ms.
Gernot Böhme, 'Non scientific traditions in higher education', in Gunnar Bergendal (ed), *Knowledge and Higher Education*, Stockholm, 1983, Almqvist & Wiksell International.

39 For this see Erika Simon, *Le Reveil populaire en Scandinavie*, Paris, 1964.

40 Chris Hurn, 'The vocationalisation of American eduation', *European Journal of Education*, vol. 18, no. 2, 1983.

Chapter 3

1 Inger Marklund, 'The impact of policy oriented education R&D', in D.B.P. Kallen et al. (eds), *Social Science Research and public policy-making: a reappraisal*, London, 1983, NFER- Nelson, p. 153.

2 Gunnar Richardson. Interview, Göteborg, November 30th 1982.

3 Aant Elzinga, 'The societal utilisation of research and development', *Paper presented to the International Political Science Association Seminar*, Haby-La Neuve (Belgium), April 21–23rd 1980, p.2.

4 See *R&D for Higher Education 1977:1*. This newsletter series, published by the NBUC, has issued reports on both

the Follow Up Programme and the Research on Higher Education Programme. Starting in the Autumn of 1983 the two programmes will, however, publish separate newsletters. The English version of the series on the Research programme will be callded *Swedish Research on Higher Education*.

5 Torsten Husén, 'Sweden' in Noel Entwistle (ed), *Strategies for Research and Development in higher education*, Amsterdam, 1976, Swets & Zeitlinger, p. 203.

6 'Research on higher education: long term development of knowledge', *R&D for Higher Education, 1983:2*, p. 4.

7 Aant Elzinga, *Science policy in Sweden: sectorialisation and adjustment to crisis*, Göteborg, March 1979, Department of the Theory of Science;
Birgitta Odén. Interview, Lund, November 24th 1982.

8 Mr Hans Löwbeer. Interview, Stockholm, November 10th 1982.

9 Lars Ekholm. Interview, Stockholm, November 4th 1982.

10 'UHA programme of research into higher education', *R&D for Higher Education 1977:8*.

11 'The Swedish programme for research into higher education', *R&D for Higher Education 1978:4*.

12 'Research into higher education; an overview', *R&D for Higher Education 1981:2*.

13 for this see Rune Premfors, 'Research and Policy-Making in Swedish Higher Education', T. Husén & M. Kogan, (eds), *Researchers and policy-makers in Education*, Oxford, 1983, Pergamon Press.

14 cf. Chapter 2, p. 17.

15 for the 'Enlightenment model' see Carol H. Weiss, 'Policy research in the context of diffuse decision-making' in Kallen *et al. op. cit.*, p. 289.

16 'The creation and support of a research community on higher education: a report to the University Chancellor's Office', *R&D for Higher Education 1977:3*.

17 *Memorandum from the Group for the Study of Higher Education and Research Policy*, Stockholm, October 20th 1982 (typewritten)

18 cf supra pp. 17–18.

19 'Research on higher education: long term development of knowledge', *R&D for Higher Education 1983:2*.
'Research on higher education: an overview', *R&D for Higher Education 1982:3*, p. 1.

20 see p. 33 for the listing of the five problem areas and *R&D for Higher Education 1982:3*, pp. 2–3.

21 *R&D for Higher Education 1983:2, op. cit.*, Table 1.

22 *ibid.*

23 *loc. cit.*, Table 2.

24 Jan Bärmark, Aant Elzinga & Göran Wallén, *Nursing care research: the emergence of a new scientific speciality*, Göteborg, 1981, Department of the Theory of Science, Report No. 127.
Jan-Erik Johansson, 'Knowledge traditions in the education of preschool teachers', *R&D for Higher Education 1981: 4.*
Lennart Svensson, 'The state and higher education: a sociological critique from Sweden', *European Journal of Education*, vol. 17, no. 3, 1982.

25 Jan-Erik Lane, Hans Stenlund & Anders Westlund, 'Variety of attitudes towards the comprehensive university', in H. Hermanns, U. Teichler & H. Wasser (Hgs), *Integrierte Hochschulmodelle*, Frankfurt/Main, 1982, Campus Verlag.
Agneta Bladh, *The trend towards vocationalism in Swedish higher education*, Stockholm, 1982, Group for the Study of Higher Education and Research Policy Report No, 21.
Jan-Erik Lane, Hans Stenlund & Anders Westlund, *Bureaucratisation of a system of higher education*, Umea, 1981, Department of Political Science Report No. 17.

26 Sigbrit Franke-Wikberg & Sten Henrysson, *Long term effects of higher education: a longitudinal study of the educational and professional 'Vorstellungen' of university students*, Umea, 1979, Department of Education.
Kjell Härnqvist, 'Long term effects of education on post secondary students', *R&D for Higher Education 1980:4*.

27 Olof Ruin, *External control and internal participation: trends in the politics and policies of Swedish higher education*, Stockholm,

1977, Group for the Study of Higher Education and Research Policy Report No. 1.

Bo Lindensjö, *The politicisation of Swedish higher education planning*, Stockholm, 1978, Department of Political Science.

Gunnar Bergendal, 'Knowledge traditions in higher education', In Bergendahl, *Knowledge and Higher Education,* op. cit.

28 J. Thelander, *Forskarutbildningen som traditionsförmedling*, Lund 1979, Deparment of History.

29 Bjorn Wittrock, 'Social knowledge, public policy and social betterment: a review of current research in knowledge utilisation in policy-making', *European Journal of Political Research,* No. 10, 1982, pp. 83–89.

Aant Elzinga, 'The social utilisation of research and development . . .' *op. cit.*, Rune Premfors, *Values and higher education policy*, Stockholm, 1982, Group for the Study of Higher Education and Research policy Report No. 18.

30 Bo Lindensjö, *The Politicisation of Swedish higher education: some views of causes, forms and effects*, Stockholm, 1978, Department of Political Science (mimeo)

Aant Elzinga, *Science policy in Sweden: sectorialisation or adjustment to crisis*, Göteborg, March 1979, Institutionen för Vetenskapsteori.

Edmund Dahlström, 'Interaction between practitioners and social science in research and development', *Research into higher education: process and structures*, Stockholm, 1979, NBUC.

31 Gunnar Bergendal. Interview, Malmö, November 23rd 1982.

32 *Svensk Forskning 1982–1986 Report No. 39-F: A report to the Government from the Council for Planning and Coordination of Research*, June 1981, pp. 94–8.

33 Maurice Kogan & Mary Henkel, *Government and research: the Rothschild experiment. A case study*, London, 1983, Heinemann.

34 'Research into higher education . . .', *R&D for Higher Education, 1982:3 op. cit.*

35 Dan Brändström. Interview, Umeå, November 18th 1982.

Chapter 4

1   Ference Marton, 'Phenomenography – describing the conceptions of the world around us', *Instructional Science*, No. 10, 1981.

2   Ference Marton. Interview, Göteborg, December 13th 1982.

3   Ference Marton, 'What does it take to learn?' in N.J. Entwistle & D. Hounsell (eds), *How Students Learn*, Lancaster, (England) 1975, Department of Educational Research.

4   Lars-Owe Dahlgren & Ference Marton, 'Students conceptions of subject matter: an aspect of learning and teaching in higher education', *Studies in Higher Education*, vol. 3, No. 1. 1978, p. 26.

5   Lars-Owe Dahlgren. Interview, Göteborg, December 28th 1982.

6   Lars-Owe Dahlgren, 'Qualitative difrences in conceptions of basic principles of economics', *Paper presented to the IVth International Conference on Higher Education*, Lancaster (England) September 1978.

7   Lennart Svensson, *Study skill and learning*, Göteborg, 1976, Göteborg Studies in Educational Sciences No. 19.

8   Lennart Svensson, 'Study skills in mechanics', *R&D for Higher Education 19-79:9.*

9   L. O. Dahlgren, 'Effects and defects of education', *Annual meeting of the Nordic Society for Educational Research,* October 1980, (typewritten).

10   Sigbrit Franke-Wikberg, 'The LONG project: an example of educational evaluation given from (sic) Sweden', *Paper presented to the I.A.E.A Conference*, Princeton (USA) 1979.

11   Sigbrit Franke-Wikberg, *Meetings between students and institutional perspectives*, Umeå, 1979 Educational Reports No. 21.

12   Lars-Owe Dahlgren & Sigbrit Franke-Wikberg, *The Social Structure of society seen through the eyes of university students*, Göteborg, 1980, Department of Education.

13 Sigbrit Franke-Wikberg. Interview, Umea November 21st 1982.

14 D. Laurillard, 'The process of student learning', *Higher Education*, No. 8, 1979. N.J. Entwistle, M. Hanley & D. Hounsell, 'Identifying distinctive approaches to studying', *ibid.*, pp. 365–380.

15 J.B. Briggs, 'Dimensions of study behaviour: another look at ATI', *British Journal of Educational Psychology*, vol. 46, 1976.

16 Guy Neave, 'On wolves and crises', *Paedagogica Europaea*, vol. xiii, No. 1, 1978, p. 20.

17 Gunnar Bergendal, 'Knowledge traditions in higher education', *R&D for Higher Education 1980:14*. Gunnar Bergendal, 'Higher education and knowledge policy: a personal view', in G. Bergendal (ed) *Knowledge and Higher Education*, Stockholm, 1983, Almqvist & Wiksell International.

18 *see supra Chapter 2*, pp. 18–19.

19 *see supra Chapter 2*, pp. 19–20.

20 Birgitta Odén, *Graduate Education in Sweden 1890–1975*, Lund, 1983, Historiska institutionen Report No. 9, MS.

21 Birgitta Odén. Interview, Lund, November 24th 1983.

22 *occ. cit.*

23 Aant Elzinga, Jan Bärmark & Göran Wallén, 'Ideologies of education and research in the health care sector', *R&D for Higher Education 1980:12*.

24 Esbjörn Johansson, 'Links with research and working life in sectorised programmes within higher education: the emergence and development of training for social workers', *R&D for Higher Education 1980:13*.

25 Bergendal, 'Knowledge traditions in higher education', *op. cit.*

26 Jan-Erik Johansson, 'Knowledge traditions in the education of pre-school teachers', *R&D for Higher Education 1981:4*.

27 Ingemar Nilsson, *The Art of medicine and medical Science* (English translation) Göteborg, 1983.

28 Ingemar Nilsson. Interview, Göteborg, January 3rd 1983.

29 Sven-Eric Liedman, 'Ideology, science and society', *R&D for Higher Education 1980:11*.

30 for example see Harry Herrmans, Ulrich Teichler & Henry Wasser, *Integrierte Hochschulmodelle – Erfahrungen aus drei Ländern*, Frankfurt/Main 1982, Campus Verlag. L. Cerych, A. Neusel, U. Teichler & H. Winkler, *The German Gesamthochschule*, Paris, 1981, Institut d'Education.

31 Robin Pedley, *The comprehensive university*, London, 1974, Allen & Unwin.

32 G.H. Bantock, *The parochialism of the present; contemporary issues in education*, London, 1981, Faber & Faber.

33 Tony Becher & Maurice Kogan, *Structure and process in higher education*, London, 1980, Heinemann. Burton C. Clark, 'Academic power: concepts, modes and perspectives', John van der Graaf (ed), *Academic power: patterns and authority in seven national systems of higher education*, New York, 1978, Praeger. Rune Premfors, *New patterns of authority in higher education*, Paris, 1981, OECD. D. Goldschmidt, 'Autonomy and accountability of higher education in the Federal Republic of Germany' in Philip G. Altbach, (ed), *The University's response to societal demands*, New York, 1975, International Council for Educational Development.

34 Runo Axelsson & Lennart Rosenberg, *Applications of organisation theory on problems of the Swedish system of higher education*, Umeå, 1976, Department of Business Administration.

35 Dominique Rivier, 'Research within the university', *European Journal of Education*, vol. 15, No. 4, 1980.

36 M. Trow, 'The public and private lives of higher education', *Daedalus*, Winter 1975.

37 Dick Ramström, Runo Axelsson & Lennart Rosenberg, 'The adaptation of university organisation into an integrated system of education', *R&D for Higher Education 1975:3*, p. 14.

38   Bertil Hammarberg & Nils Hägg-ström, *Adult and non traditional education and the regional dimension*, Umea, 1978, Geografiska institutionen Rapport No. C38.

39   Jan-Erik Lane, 'The university as an organisation: system and environ-ment', *Educational Development 1976:7*, p. 3.

40   Jan-Erik Lane, *Higher education in Scandinavia in a comparative perspective*, Umea, November 1981, Statsvetenskapliga in-stitionen Forskningsrapport 1981:15 (mimeo).

41   *ibid.*, p. 14.

42   Jan-Erik Lane, 'Power in the Univer-sity' *European Journal of Education*, vol. 14, No. 4, 1979.

43   viz Becher & Kogan, *op. cit.*

44   Burton C. Clark, *Academic power in Italy: bureaucracy and oligarchy in a national university system*, Chicago, 1977, Chi-cago University Press.

45   Staffan Gran, *Innovationshinder inom Hög-skolan*, Göteborg, 1981, Företagseko-nomiska institutionen.

46   Agneta Bladh, *The trend towards voca-tionalism in Swedish higher education*, Stockholm, May 1982, Group for the Study of Higher Education and Re-search Policy, Report No. 16.

47   Jan-Erik Lane, Hans Stenlund & An-ders Westlund, *Bureaucratisation of a sys-tem of higher education*, Umeå December 1981, Statsvetenskapliga institutionen (mimeo) p. 11.

48   Dominique Rivier, 'La gestion de l'uni-versite contemporaine: planification et décentralisation', *CRE Information*, No. 44, 4th Quarter 1978, pp. 55–56.

49   Wilhelm Hennis, 'The legislation and the German university', *Minerva*, Vol. 15, 1977, p. 305.

50   R.J. Kuiper, 'How democratic is the Dutch university?' in S. Armstrong (ed), *A Decade of change*, Guildford (Eng-land) 1979, Society for Research into Higher Education, pp. 78–80.

51   Jan-Erik Lane, 'Public administration and organisational development: Swe-dish higher education in the light of six theoretical models', *European Journal of Education*, vol. 15, No. 3, 1980.

52   A.H. Halsey & Martin Trow, *The Brit-ish Academics*, London, 1971, Faber & Faber.

53   Jan-Erik Lane, Hans Stenlund & An-ders Westlund, 'Variety of attitudes to-wards the comprehensive university', *Higher Education*, Vol. 11, 1982, pp. 441–474.

54   Lennart Svensson, 'From cultivation to education: a study of the develop-ment of the Swedish university from a traditional cultural institution to a ra-tional educational institution', *R&D for Higher Education 1980:9*, p. 2.

55   *ibid.*, pp. 5–6.
     Bengt Gesser, 'Rationalisation: know-ledge, function, reproduction and Swe-dish universities', (English transla-tion), *Forskning om Utbildning*, No. 4, 1979.
     Lennart Svensson, 'The state and higher education: a sociological cri-tique from Sweden', *European Journal of Education*, vol. 17, no. 3, 1982.

56   Svensson, 'The State and higher edu-cation', *op. cit.*, p. 295.

57   Svensson, 'From cultivation to educa-tion . . . *op. cit.*, p. 9.

58   Guy Neave, 'La notion de limites com-me model des liens existant entre l'université et l'Etat', *CRE Information*, No. 58, 1982.

59   Gesser, 'Rationalisation . . .', *op. cit.*

60   Lane, 'Public administration and or-ganisational development', *op. cit.*

61   for this aspect in Britain see Rowland Eustace, 'British higher education and the State', *European Journal of Education*, vol. 17, No. 3, 1982, pp. 283 ff.

62   Notker Hammarstein, 'University de-velopment from the 16th to the 18th centuries: a comparative perspective', *Paper presented to the Conference The Changing social function of the European University*, Berne, March 1983.

63   Hans Reiss (ed), *Emmanual Kant: poli-tical writings*, Cambridge, 1977, CUP.

64 Laetitia Boehme, 'Humboldt and the university: idea and implementation', *Paper presented to the Conference The Changing Social Function. . . op. cit.*

65 Mark Pattison, *Memoires*, Oxford 1895, quoted in Eustace, *op. cit.*

66 Guy Neave, *Patterns of Equality; the influence of new structures in European higher education upon equality of opportunity*, Windsor (England) 1976, NFER–Nelson.
Jean-Pierre Jallade, 'Expenditure on higher education in Europe', *European Journal of Education*, vol. 15, no. 1, 1980; Reinhard Reise, *Die Hochschule auf dem Wege zum wissenschaftlichen Grossbetrieb*, Stuttgart, 1977, Klett Verlag.
Lyman Glenny (ed), *Funding higher education: a six nation analysis* New York, 1979, Praeger.
Michel Hecquet, 'Procédures et mecanismes d'allocation', *Bulletin de l'Observatoire de la Gestion universitaire*, No. 1, December 1982, pp. 19–21.

67 Guy Neave, 'On the edge of the abyss', *European Journal of Education* Vol. 17, No. 1, 1982.

68 Hans Daalder & Edward Shils (eds) *Universities, Politicians and Bureaucrats*, Cambridge, 1982, CUP.

69 Rune Premfors, *The Politics of higher education in a comparative perspective: France, Sweden and the United Kingdom*, Stockholm, 1980, Stockholm Studies in Politics No. 15.

70 Bo Lindensjö, *The Politicisation of Swedish higher education planning* Stockholm, 1978, Department of Political Science (mimeo)

71 Lillemor Kim, *Widened admission to higher education in Sweden – the 25/5 scheme: a study of the implementation process*, Stockholm, 1982, National Board of Universities and Colleges, pp. 70–71.

72 for the latter point see George A Kelly, 'Who needs a theory of citizenship?', *Daedalus*, vol. 118, No. 4, Fall 1979.

73 Rune Premfors, 'The politics of higher education in Sweden: recent developments 1976–1978', *European Journal of Education*, vol. 14, No. 1, 1979.

74 *ibid*.

75 Rune Premfors, *Integrated higher education: the Swedish perspective*, Stockholm, June 1981, Group for the Study of Higher Education and Research Policy. See also Hermans, Teichler & Wasser (eds) *Integrierte Hochschulmodelle*, *op. cit.*, pp. 127– 144.

76 Rune Premfors, Social Research and governmental commissions in Sweden, *American Behavioural Scientist*, vol. 26, No. 5 May-June 1983.

77 Bo Lindensjö, *Higher Education Reform: a study of public reform strategy*, Stockholm, 1981, Stockholm Studies in Politics No. 20.

78 Bo Lindensjö, 'U68 – a study of the origins of the reform of higher education', *R&D for Higher Education 1982:4*, p. 7.

79 Bo Lindensjö, *Higher education reform . . . op. cit.*

80 Bo Lindensjö, *The politicisation of Swedish higher education planning: some views on causes, forms and effects*, Stockholm, 1978, Department of Political Science (mimeo).

81 Lindensjö, 'U68 – a study of the origins . . .' *op. cit.*, p. 9.

82 *ibid*.

83 Lindensjö, *Higher education reform: a study of public strategy, op. cit.*

84 Boehme, *op. cit.*

85 Guy Neave, 'Academic drift; some views from Europe', *Studies in Higher Education*, Vol. 6, No. 2, 1979.

86 Stuart S. Blume, 'The finance of university research in Europe', *European Journal of Education*, Vol. 15, No. 4, 1980, p. 377.

87 Professor Erik Lönnroth. Interview, Göteborg, January 10th 1983. Blume, *op. cit.*, p. 378.

88 'The structure of studies and place of research in mass higher education', *Conference on future structures of post secondary Education*, Paris, 1974, OECD.

89 *Science, growth and society*, Paris, 1971, OECD, quoted in Bjorn Wittrock, 'Science policy and the challenge to the welfare state', *West European Politics*, Vol. 3, No. 3, October 1980.

90 Edmond Lisle, *Social Science research in the United Kingdom*, Paris, 1983, Maison des Sciences de l'Homme (mimeo)

91 Hans Landberg. Interview, Stockholm, November 2nd 1982.

92 Wittrock, *op. cit.*, p. 364.

93 Rune Premfors, 'The politics of higher education in Sweden: recent developments 1976–1978', *European Journal of Education*, vol. 14, No. 1, 1979, p. 101.

94 Stuart S. Blume, *Science policy research*, Stockholm, 1981, Swedish Council for planning and coordination of research.

95 cf Edmund Dahlström, 'Researchers, practitioners and the development of social science', *R&D for Higher Education 1977:5*.

96 cf Björn Wittrock, 'R&D and public policy-making', *R&D for Higher Education 1980:2*.

97 Björn Wittrock, 'Social knowledge, public policy and social betterment: a review of current research on knowledge utilisation in policy-making', *European Journal of Political Research*, No. 10, 1982, p. 10.

98 Aant Elzinga, ' "Science studies" in Sweden', *Social Studies of Science*, Vol. 10, May 1980, p. 197.

99 Aant Elzinga, *The Societal utilisation of R&D*, Göteborg, April 1980, Department of the Theory of Science Report No. 58 Series 2 (xerox) p. 12.

100 Rune Premfors, *Numbers and beyond, access policy in an international perspective*, Stockholm, March 1982, Group for the Study of Higher Education and Research Policy Report No. 20, pp. 22–3. also,
Journal of Higher Education (forthcoming 1983).

101 Aant Elzinga, *Science policy in Sweden: sectorisation or adjustment to crisis*, Göteborg, March 1979, Institutionen för Vetenskapsteori, (mimeo)

102 for this see supra p. 39.

103 Björn Wittrock. Interview, Stockholm, November 12th 1982.

104 Rune Premfors. Interview, Stockholm, November 15th 1982.

105 Wittrock, 'Science policy and the challenge to the welfare state', *op. cit.*, Björn Wittrock & Kent Zetterberg, 'Implementation beyond hierarchy Swedish energy research policy', *European Journal of Political Research*, Vol. 10, No. 2, 1982.

106 Rune Premfors & Björn Wittrock, 'Research and development for higher education in Sweden: some conceptual and policy problems', in *Research into higher education: processes and structures*, Stockholm, 1979, National Board of Universities and Colleges.

107 *ibid.*

108 Rune Premfors, 'Research and policy-making in Swedish higher education', in T. Husén & M. Kogan (eds) *Researchers and policy-makers in Education*, Oxford, 1983, Pergamon Press.

109 *ibid.*, p. 44.

110 *loc. cit.*

111 Rune Premfors, 'The use of sectoral research', *R&D for Higher Education 1982:1*, pp. 9–11.

112 Elzinga, ' "Science studies" in Sweden', *op. cit.*, p. 200

Chapter 5

1 Maurice Kogan & Mary Henkel, *Government and Research. The Rothschild experiment: a case study*, London, 1983, Heinemann.

2 Chancellor Carl-Gustaf Andrén. Interview, Stockholm, November 9th 1982. Guy Neave & Ladislav Cerych, *Structure, promotion and advancement in the academic profession: France, the Netherlands, the United Kingdom and the United States. Report presented to the Volkswagenstiftung*, Paris, March 1981, (mimeo) Institut Europeen d'Education et de Politique Sociale.

3 Ulrich Teichler, 'Recent development in higher education in the Federal Republic of Germany', *European Journal of Education*, vol. 17, No. 2, 1982, p. 167.

4 Hans Skoie, *Ageing university staff*, Oslo, 1976, Institute for Studies in Research and Higher Education.

5 Guy Neave, 'Mobility is the key to France's future', *Times Higher Education Supplement*, January 29th 1982.

6 Erland Ringborg. Interview, Stockholm, November 4th 1982.

7 Tony Becher, 'Britain' in Noel Entwistle (ed), *Strategies for research and development in higher education*, Amsterdam/Lisse, 1976, Swets & Zeitlinger.

8 Brief for the Minister from the Society for Research into Higher Education, November 11th 1982, (typewritten) p. 5.

9 *ibid.*, p. 7.

10 Howard Machin, *The CNRS and social science research in France*, (memorandum) London, May 1982, (mimeo) p. 13.

11 *ibid.*

12 *Rapport sur l'Emploi scientifique*, Paris, 1979, La Documentation Française. (Massenet Report)

13 *La Réforme du financement des universités*, Paris, 1981, La Documentation Française. (Freville Report)

Chapter 6

1 For this see the booklet containing a series of articles by Hans-Magnus Enzensberger, 'Svensk Höst', *Dagens Nyheter*, December 1982.

2 But see Professor Nils Runeby's project in progress dealing with Student Organisations 1945–1965.

3 See supra p. 64.

4 Guy Neave, 'Regional development and higher education', *Higher Education Review*, vol. 14, No. 3, Summer 1979.
   Guy Neave, 'Higher education and regional development: an overview of a growing controversy', *European Journal of Education*, vol. 14, No. 3, 1979.

Appendices

The purpose of these appendices is to provide information concerning essential and useful sources for researchers and scholars interested in the field of Higher Education in Sweden.

Appendix 1 comprises a list of publications resulting from the Programme for Research into Higher Education. A criterion for selection has been that the materials cited are either books or journals generally available to users of national or university libraries. Also included are Ph.D dissertations.

Appendix 2 comprises a select list of on-going projects being conducted within the framework of this Programme whose researchers will provide further information about work in progress.

Two other sources are: *Swedish Research on Higher Education* (earlier called *R&D for Higher Education*) – a newsletter series in English – and *UHÄ-Rapport*, in Swedish. Both are published by the National Board of Universities and Colleges and obtainable on request from the Research on Higher Education Programme, NBUC, P.O. Box 45501, S-104 30 Stockholm, Sweden.

Appendix 1

Selected bibliography of publications resulting from
the Programme for Research into
Higher Education 1973–1983

Higher education in society

Abrahamsson, Kenneth (1974) *Kom igen, Svensson! Om vuxenutbildningens kommunikationsproblem* (Lund: Studentlitteratur)

Abrahamsson, Kenneth (1976) *The Need for a Dialogue. On the counselling needs of presumptive adult learners in higher education*, Department of Education, Stockholm University, (Ph D dissertation)

Abrahamsson, Kenneth & Edfeldt Åke W (1976) *Den svåra dialogen. Om kontakten mellan högskolan och presumtiva vuxenstuderande* (Lund: Studentlitteratur)

Bengtsson, Jarl & Bengtsson, Monica (1975) *Recurrent Education. Some Observations and a Bibliography* (Stockholm University Chancellor's Office, UKÄ-Report, 1975:8).

Berner, Boel (1981) *Teknikens värld. Teknisk förändring och ingenjörsarbete i svensk industri (The World of Technique. Technical Change and Technical Labour in Swedish Industry)* (Lund: Arkiv avhandlingsserie 11) (PhD dissertation; English Summary)

Berner, Boel (1982) 'Kvinnor, kunskap och makt i teknikens värld', *Kvinnovetenskaplig Tidskrift*, Nr 3

Brennan, J & Franke-Wikberg, Sigbrit (1980) 'The socialization outcome of Higher Education: Some Problems of Methodology', *International Social Council*, Vienna Centre, Doc. No 92, App. 7, Oct. 1980

Dahlgren, Lars Owe (1983) 'Higher Education – Impact on Students', in Husén, Torsten & Postlethwaite, T N (Eds.) *International Encyclopedia of Education. Research and Studies* (London: Pergamon Press).

Dahlgren, Lars Owe (Forthcoming) 'The Outcome of Learning', in Marton, Ference, Entwistle, N J & Hounsell, D *The Experience of Learning* (Edinburgh: Scottish Academic Press)

Dahlgren, Lars-Owe, Gibbs, G & Hounsell, D (Forthcoming) 'Understanding Learning and Teaching for Understanding', in Marton, Ference, Entwistle, N J & Hounsell, D (eds) *The Experience of Learning* (Edinburgh: Scottish Academic Press)

Dahllöf, Urban (1975) 'Problems and pitfalls in assessing internal efficiency in higher education by means of mass statistics. Some experiences from Sweden', *Scandinavian Journal of Educational Research*, Vol 19, pp. 175–189.

Dahllöf, Urban (1977) *Reforming Higher Education and External Studies in Sweden and Australia* (Stockholm: Almqvist & Wiksell International)

Ekehammar, Bo (1977) 'Intelligence and Social Background as Related to Psychological Cost-Benefit in Career Choice', *Psychological Reports*, Vol 40, pp. 963–970.

Ekehammar, Bo (1977) 'Test of a Psychological Cost-Benefit Model for Career Choice', *Journal of Vocational Behaviour*, Vol 10, pp. 245–260.

Ekehammar, Bo (1978) 'Psychological Cost-Benefit as an Intervening Construct in Career Choice Models', *Journal of Vocational Behaviour*, Vol 12, 1978, pp. 279–289.

Elgqvist-Saltzman, Inga (1976) *Vägen genom universitetet (The Way through the University)* (Stockholm: Almqvist & Wiksell International (Ph D dissertation; English Summary).

Fasth Eva (1980) *Aspekter på utlokalisering av högre utbildning (Aspects of Relocalisation of Higher Education)*, (PhD dissertation) (Lund: Tryckbaren) (English Summary)

Franke-Wikberg, Sigbrit & Henrysson, Sten (1979) 'A Study of Higher Education and "Vorstellungen" of Students', *International Social Science council*, Vienna Centra, Doc. No 69.

Franke-Wikberg, Sigbrit & Zetterström, Bo-Olof (1983) 'From Ideas on Quality of Education to Ideas as Quality of Education', in Framhein, Gerhild & Langer, Josef (Eds.) *Student und Studium in Internationalen Vergleich* (Klagenfurt: Kärntner Universitäts Druckerei).

Gesser, Bengt (1977) 'Campanella och AMS – manuellt och mentalt arbete i yrkesvägledning', *Sociologisk Forskning*, Nr 2–3.

Gesser, Bengt (1977) 'Skolsystem och social skiktning', in Lundberg, Svante, Selander, Steffan & Höglund, Ulf *Jämlikhet och klassherravälde* (Lund: Bo Cavefors bokförlag)

Gesser, Bengt (1978) 'Studenter: utbildning och politik', *Forskning om utbildning*, Nr 2.

Gesser, Bengt (1979) 'Rationalisering: kunskap, funktionsreproduktion och svenska universitet', *Forskning om utbildning*, Nr 4.

Gesser, Bengt & Fasth, Eva (1973) *Gymnasieutbildning och social skiktning* (Stockholm: UKÄ)

Hellberg, Inga (1978) *Studier i professionell organisation. En professionsteori med tillämpning på veterinäryrket (Studies in Professional Organization. A Theory of Professions with Application to the Veterinary Profession)*, Department of Sociology, Göteborg University, Monograph No 20 (PhD dissertation; English Summary).

Idman, Pekka (1974) *Equality and Democracy. Studies of Teacher Training* (PhD dissertation) (Lund: CWK Gleerup).

Johansson, L (1975) 'Vuxenutbildning och jämlikhet', in *Årsbok för vuxenutbildning* (Malmö 1975/6)

Johansson, L & Ekerwald, H (1976) *Vuxenstudier och livssituation* (Stockholm, Bokförlaget Prisma)

Lindensjö, Bo (1983) 'Sverige i olag? Allmänintresset under omprövning', *Häften för kritiska studier*, Nr 2, s 3–14.

Lindensjö, Bo & Lundgren, Ulf (1983) 'Att utvärdera utvärdering', *Forskning om utbildning*, Nr 2.

Magnusson, David, (1978) 'A Longitudinal Investigation of Development and Adjustment. The Örebro Project', in Dunér, A (Ed:) *Research into Personal Development: Educational and Vocational Choice* (Amsterdam and Lisse: Swets & Zeitlinger).

Magnusson, David &Dunér, Anders (1978) 'The Örebro Project: A Longitudinal Study of Individual Development and Adjustment', in Mednick, S (Ed.) *Survey on Prospective Longitudinal Research in Europe with Direct or Indirect Implications for Mental Health* (Copenhagen: WHO, Regional Office of Europe).

Magnusson, David & Dunér, Anders (1978) 'Enquète longitudinale sur le développement et l'adaption', *Annales de Vaucresson*, Vol 15, pp. 89–110.

Magnusson, David (1979) 'Methodology and Strategy Problems in Longitudinal Research', in Schulsinger, F & Mednick, S (Eds.) *Proceedings from a Seminar on Longitudinal Research in Aarhus* (Oxford University Press).

Magnusson, David, Dunér, Anders & Zetterblom, Göran (1975) *Adjustment – a Longitudal Study. The Örebro Project* (Stockholm: Almqvist & Wiksell, New York: Wiley).

Mählck, Lars (1980) *Choice of Post-secondary Studies in a Stratified System of Education – A Swedish Follow-up Study'* (Stockholm: Almqvist & Wiksell International) (PhD dissertation).

Nilsson, Anders (1977) 'Study Financing and Expansion of Education', *Economy and History*, Vol 10, No 2, pp. 92–113.

Nilsson, Anders (1983) *Studiefinansiering och social rekrytering till högre utbildning 1920–1977* (Lund: Studentlitteratur) (PhD dissertation, English summary)

Ohlsson, Rolf (1981) 'Invandring och högskoleexpansion. Utländska studenter i det svenska högskoleväsendet', *Historisk Tidskrift*, Nr 2, s 183–191.

Ohlsson, Rolf (1983) *Högre utbildning, konjunkturer och demografiska förändringar* (Lund: Studentlitteratur)

Pettersson, Lars (1977) 'Some Aspects of the Expansion of Education in Sweden', *Economy and History*, Vol 10, No 2, pp. 69–91.

Pettersson, Lars (1981) 'Kapitalbildning och utbildning. Om ingenjörsutbildningens dimensionering', *Historisk tidskrift*, Nr 2, s 192–200.

Pettersson, Lars (1983) *Ingenjörsutbildning och kapitalbildning 1933–1973* (Lund: Studentlitteratur) (PhD dissertation, English summary).

Sohlman, Åsa (1981) *Labour Market and Human Capital Models. Swedish Experiences and Theoretical Analyses*, (Department of Political Economy, Stockholm University (PhD dissertation).

Sohlman, Åsa (1982) *Utbildning och arbetsmarknad* (Lund: Studentlitteratur).

Higher education as an organization

Axelsson, R & Rosenberg, L (1974) 'Towards a new university organisation', *Higher Education*, vol 3.

Axelsson, R & Rosenberg, L (1975) 'Universitetsorganisatoriska utvecklingsproblem', *Ekonomisk Debatt*, Nr 3, s 188–196.

Axelsson, Runo & Rosenberg, Lennart (1976) *Applications of Organization Theory. On Problems of the Swedish system of Higher Education*, Department of Business Administration, Umeå University, Report No 4. (PhD dissertation).

Bärmark, Jan & Wallén, Göran (1980) 'Vårdutbildningarnas forskningsanknytning från praxis till forskning', *Tidskrift för sjukvårdspedagoger*, Nr 5/6.

Bärmark, J & Elzinga, A & Wallén, G (1981) 'Omvårdnadsforskning, vetenskap och beprövad erfarenhet', *Sjukgymnasten*, nr 8/9.

Cigéhn, Göran (1976) *Förändringar i partipolitiska sympatier och utbildningsval under studietiden* (Changes in Party Political Affiliation and the Choice of Field of Study among Students), Department of Sociology, Umeå University, Report No 26. (PhD dissertation).

Fredriksson, Bert (1980) *Högskolans basenheter. Norm och verklighet (The Basic Units of Higher Education. Norm and Reality)*, Umeå Studies in Politics and Administration, No 3, Umeå University (English Summary) (PhD dissertation).

Gran, Staffan (1981) *Innovationshinder i högskolan (Obstacles to Innovation in Higher Education)*, Department of Business Economics, Göteborg University (English Summary) (PhD dissertation).

Hammarberg, Bertil & Häggström, Nils (1979) 'Education and Regional Development', *General Report*, Vol I, OECD, Paris.

Hammarberg, Bertil & Häggström, Nils (1979) 'Education and Regional Development', *Technical Reports*, Vol II, OECD, Paris.

Hammarberg, Bertil et al (1979) 'Regional Effects of Swedish Educational Planning', *Educational and Regional Development*, (Paris: OECD).

Herbert, A & Molander, S (1975) *Prefekten i arbete: en explorativ studie av ledningsfunktionen vid universitets- och högskoleinstitutioner* (Stockholm: Information från PTI, Nr 75).

Kilander, Svenbjörn (1983) 'Staten byter ansikte', in Abrahamsson, K & Ramström, D (red) *Vägen till planrike. Om stat, sektor och sammanhang* (Lund: Studentlitteratur).

Kim, Lillemor (1982) *Widened Admission to Higher Education in Sweden – the 25/5 scheme – A Study of the Implementation Process* (Stockholm: National Board of Universities and Colleges).

Lane, Jan-Erik (1977) 'Some Theoretical Notes on Institutional Autonomy', *Statsvetenskaplig Tidskrift*, No 4, pp. 247–257.

Lane, Jan-Erik (1978) 'Interpreting Higher Education Institutions: In order to find keep searching, but search where you may find!', *Statsvetenskaplig Tidskrift*, No 3.

Lane, Jan-Erik (1979) 'Power in the University', *European Journal of Education*, Vol 14.

Lane, Jan-Erik (1979) 'Yes, budgetary analysis may be conducted in accordance with Scientific Method', *Statsvetenskaplig Tidskrift*, No 4.

Lane, Jan-Erik (1979) 'The Budgetary Process in Swedish Higher Education', in Glenny, L (Ed.) *Funding Higher Education: A Six Nation Analysis* (New York: Praeger).

Lane, Jan-Erik (1980) 'Public Administration and Organizational Development; Swedish higher education in the light of six theoretical models', *European Journal of Education*, Vol 15, No 3, pp. 299–311.

Lane, Jan-Erik (1981) 'University Autonomy: A New Analysis'', *Vestes, The Australian Universities' Review*, Vol 24, No 1, pp. 17–27.

Lane, Jan-Erik (1981) 'Om byråkrati och högskolans byråkratisering', *Tvärsnitt*, No 1.

Lane, Jan-Erik (1981) 'Tjänster och förvaltning i högskolan', *Tvärsnitt*, No 2.

Lane, Jan-Erik (1981) 'Den statliga högskolans struktur', *Tvärtsnitt*, No. 4.

Lane, Jan-Erik (1982) 'Das Hochschulwesen in Skandinavien in einer vergleichenden Übersicht', in Huert, L (Ed.) *Europäischen Encyclopedie Erziehungswissenschaft* (Hamburg: Klett-Kotta Verlag).

Lane, Jan-Erik (1983) *Creating the University of Norland. Goals, Structures and Outcomes*, Umeå Studies in Politics and Administration, No 7. (Lund: CWK Gleerup).

Lane, Jan-Erik (1983) 'Higher Education, Policy-Making and Implemantation', *Higher Education*, vol 12.

Lane, Jan-Erik (1983) 'The Higher Education Profession in Sweden. Structure, Flexibility and Equality', *European Journal of Education*, Vol 18, No. 3.

Lane, Jan-Erik & Fredriksson, Bert (1983) *Higher Education and Public Administration* (Stockholm: Almqvist & Wiksell International).

Lane, Jan-Erik (forthcoming) 'Academic Profession in Academic Organization', *Higher Education*, vol 13.

Lane, Jan-Erik (forthcoming) 'Power', in Sartori, G (Ed.) *Social Science Concepts* (Beverly Hills: Sage).

Lane, Jan-Erik, Stenlund, Hans & Westlund, Anders (1981) 'Is There a University Crisis in Sweden? A Survey of National Academic Opinion', *European Journal of Education*, Vol 16, Nos 3-4.

Lane, Jan-Erik, Stenlund, Hans & Westlund, Anders (1982) 'Variety of Attitudes towards the Comprehensive University', *Higher Education*, Vol 11, 1982, and in Hermanns, H, Teichler, U & Wasser, H (Hg.) *Integrierte Hochschulmodelle* (Frankfurt: Campus).

Lane, Jan-Erik, Stenlund, Hans (1983) 'Bureaucratization of a System of Higher Education', *Comparative Education*, vol 19.

Lindensjö, Bo (1978) 'Jürgen Habermas och Claus Offes statsteori', *Häften för kritiska studier*, No 6.

Lindensjö, Bo (1979) 'Politisk planering – verklighet eller myt?', *Häften för kritiska studier*, No 6.

Lindensjö, Bo (1981) *Högskolereformen. En studie i offentlig reformstrategi (Higher Education Reform. A Study of Public Reform Strategy)*. Stockholm Studies in Politics, No 20 (English Summary, PhD dissertation).

Lindensjö, Bo (1981) 'Statsinterventionism och högskolepolitik. Exemplet U68', *Häften för Kritiska Studier*, Nr 5-6.

Lindensjö, Bo (1983) 'Den segmenterade staten', i Abrahamsson, K, Ramström, D (red), *Vägen till Planrike. Om stat, sektor och sammanhang* (Lund: Studentlitteratur).

Nilsson, Ingemar (1981) 'Testning och klinisk psykologi', *Kritisk psykologi*, Nr 1, s 4-25.

Nilsson, Ingemar ((1983) 'Medicinen som profession under 1700-talet', *Sociologisk forskning*, Nr 2, s 3-15.

Premfors, Rune (1979) 'The Politics of Higher Education in Sweden: Recent Developments 1976-1978', *European Journal of Education*, Vol 14, 1.

Premfors, Rune (1980) *The Politics of Higher Education in a Comparative Perspective: France, Sweden, the United Kingdom*, Stockholm Studies in Politics no 15, Department of Political Science, Stockholm University. (PhD dissertation)

Premfors, Rune (1981) *New Patterns of Authority in Higher Education* (Paris: OECD).

Premfors, Rune (1981) Review Article: Charles Lindblom and Aaron Wildavsky, *British Journal of Political Science*, Vol 11 (April).

Premfors, Rune (1981) 'National Policy Styles and Higher Education in France, Sweden and the United Kingdom', *European Journal of Education*, Vol 16, 2.

Premfors, Rune & Östergren, Bertil (1978) *Systems of Higher Education: Sweden* (New York: International Council for Educational Development).

Ramström, Dick (1977) 'Styrning- och beslutsproblem i den nya högskolan', *UHÄ-rapport*, 1977:20, s 95–126.

Svensson, Lennart G (1978) *Från bildning till utbildning. Del I. En diskussion kring historie- och sociologisk teori om universitetens utveckling och omvandling*, Sociologiska institutionen, Göteborgs universitet, monografi nr 17.

Svensson, Lennart G (1978) *Från bildning till utbildning. Del II. Universitetens omvandling från 1100-talet till 1870-talet*, Sociologiska institutionen, Göteborgs universitet, monografi nr 18.

Svensson, Lennart G (1980) *Från bildning till utbildning. Del III. Universitetens omvandling från 1870 till 1970 (From Bildung to Ausbildung. Changes in Swedish Universities from 1870 to 1970)*, Department of Sociology, Göteborg University, Monograph No 21 (English Summary; PhD dissertation).

Svensson, Lennart (1982) 'The State and Higher Education. A sociological critique from Sweden', *European Journal of Education*, Vol 17, No 3.

The Research Function

Abrahamsson, Bengt (1977) 'Forskningsanknytning. Om sambandet mellan forskning och utbildning', *UHÄ-rapport*, 1977:20, s 127–147.

Andolf, Göran (1980) *Dålig och bra historia. Fakultetsopponenternas recensioner av doktorsavhandlingar i historia 1890–1975*, Historiska institutionen, Lunds universitet, delrapport 2.

Bergsten, Karl-Erik (1980) *Forskartraditioner i kulturgeografi vid svenska universitet under 1900-talet*, Historiska institutionen, Lunds universitet, delrapport 5.

Bengtsson, Margot (1980) 'Varför blir somliga kvinnor naturvetare och inte humanister?' *Kvinnovetenskaplig tidskrift*, Nr 2.

Bengtsson, Margot (1983) *Föräldraidentifikation hos kvinnliga naturvetare och humanister. Utvecklingspsykologiska, differentiella och socialpsykologiska aspekter*, Institutionen för tillämpad psykologi, Lunds universitet (English Summary; PhD dissertation).

Bertilsson, Margareta (1980) 'Sociologin inför 1980-talet. En blågul sociologi', *Sociologisk forskning*, Nr 1, s 27–32.

Blom, C, Pikwer, B (1976) *Vem blev forskare och vad blev forskaren? En studie av de forskarutbildade i ämnena historia, statskunskap, kulturgeografi och ekonomisk historia 1890–1970*, Historiska institutionen, Lunds universitet, delrapport 1.

Blom, Conny (1980) *Doktorsavhandlingarna i historia 1890–1975*, Historiska institutionen, Lunds universitet, delrapport 8.

Bärmark, Jan & Wallén, Göran (1980) 'The Development of an Interdisciplinary Project. The Social Process of Scientific Investigation', *Sociology of Sciences*, Vol IV, pp. 221–235.

Dahllöf, Urban (1980) 'Småplotter eller perspektiv mot framtiden?' *Tvärsnitt*, Nr 1.

Dahllöf, Urban (1982) 'Den rika systern eller Askungen?', *Tvärsnitt*, Nr 2.

Dahlström, Edmund (1979) 'Interaction between practitioners and social scientists in reserch and development', in *Research into Higher Education: Processes and Structures* (Stockholm: National Board of Universities and Colleges), pp. 237-278.

Dahlström, Edmund (1980) *Samhällsvetenskap och praktik. Studier i samhällelig kunskapsutveckling* (Stockholm: Liber)

Dahlström, Edmund (1980) 'Samhällsvetenskap och praktik', *UHÄ-rapport*, 1980:14, pp. 1-6.

Elzinga, Aant (1979) 'The Sectorization Principle in Swedish Science Policy', in Pfetsch, F R (Ed.) *Internationale Dimensionen in der Wissenschaft* (Erlangen: Institut für Gesellschaft und Wissenschaft).

Elzinga, Aant (1980) 'Science Policy in Sweden: Sectorization and adjustment to crisis', *Research Policy*, Vol 9, pp. 116-146.

Elzinga, Aant (1980) 'Vetenskapen i samhället. Några perspektiv och problemställningar', *UHÄ-rapport*, 1980:14, s 85-117.

Elzinga, Aant (1980) 'Science Studies in Sweden. Country Report', *Social Studies of Science*, Vol 10, pp. 181-214.

Elzinga, Aant (1983) 'Forskningspolitiken och den liberala korporativismen', *Sociologisk forskning*, Nr 4, s 39-63.

Elzinga, Aant (forthcoming) 'The Growth of Science: Technocratic and Romatic Images', in Tord Ganelius (ed) *Scientific Progress and its Social Conditions* (London: Pergamon Press).

Elzinga, Aant (forthcoming) 'Review of Barry Barnes, Kuhn and the Social Sciences', *Acta Sociologica*, vol 27.

Fridjonsdottir, Katrin (1983) *Vetenskap och politik. En kunskapssociologisk studie* (Lund: Akademilitteratur) (English Summary; PhD dissertation).

Hettne, Björn (1980) *Ekonomisk historia i Sverige. En översikt av vetenskaplig produktion och forskningsinriktning*, Historiska institutionen, Lunds universitet, delrapport 4.

Husén, Torsten (1975) *Universiteten och forskningen*, (Stockholm: Natur och Kultur).

Husén, Torsten (1976-77) 'Swedish University Research at the Crossroads', *Minerva*, Vol 14, No 4, pp. 419-446.

Husén, Torsten (1977) 'Ausbildung und Forschung im Widerspruch', *Neue Sammlung*, Vol 17, Heft 6, November/Dezember, pp. 521-537.

Husén, Torsten (1979) 'Universitetsforskningen i kris', *Tiden*, Nr 9, pp. 501-509.

Johansson, Esbjörn (1979) *Sektoriell kunskapsutveckling*, Sociologiska institutionen, Göteborgs universitet, report No 56.

Johansson, Esbjörn (1981) *UHÄ:s FoU-verksamhet. Del I.* Sociologiska institutionen, Göteborgs universitet, report No 67.

Johansson, Leif (1980) *Forskning om politik. En studie av doktorsavhandlingarna i statskunskap 1890-1975*, Historiska institutionen, Lunds universitet, delrapport 6.

Odén, Birgitta (1973) 'Historia som forskningsprocess', *Scandia*, Nr 2, pp. 151-158.

Odén, Birgitta (1975) *Lauritz Weibull och forskarsamhället*, (Lund: CWK Geerup).

Odén, Birgitta (1975) 'Det moderna historisk-kritiska genombrottet i svensk historisk forskning', *Scandia*, Nr 1, pp. 5–29.

Odén, Birgitta (1980) 'Forskande kvinnor inom svensk historievetenskap', *Historisk tidskrift*, pp. 244–265.

Odén, Birgitta (1981) 'Överföring av värderingar genom forskarutbildning', i *Vardag och evighet, Festskrift till Hampus Lyttkens*,(Lund: Doxa). pp. 197–209.

Pikwer, Birgitta (1980) *Bibliografi över licentiat- och doktorsavhandlingar i historia 1890–1975*, Historiska institutionen, Lunds universitet, delrapport 7.

Premfors, Rune (1979) 'Research and Development for Higher Education. Report from Discussion Group 5'. In *Research into Higher Education: Processes and Structures* (Stockholm: National Board of Universities and Colleges).

Premfors, Rune (1979) 'Social Research and Public Policy Making: An Overview', *Statsvetenskaplig Tidskrift*, No 4.

Premfors, Rune (1980) 'Review of D K Price, The Scientific Estate', *British Journal of Political Science*, vol 11, 2.

Premfors, Rune (1982) 'Values and Higher Education Policy', *Policy Sciences*, 14 (1982), pp. 365–378.

Premfors, Rune (1982) 'The Pursuit of Efficency and Effectiveness in Swedish Government', in *Appendices to the Third Report from the Treasury and Civil Service Committee*, Annex 3, Memorandum, pp. 70–83 (London: HMSO).

Premfors, Rune (1983) 'Analysis in Politics: The Regionalization of Swedish Higher Education', *Comparative Education Review*, vol 27.

Premfors, Rune (1983) 'Numbers and Beyond: Access Policy in an International Perspective', *Journal of Higher Education*, Vol 54.

Premfors, Rune (1983) 'Research and Policy-Making in Swedish Higher Education', in T Husén and M Kogan (Eds.) *Researchers and Policy Makers in Education* (Oxford: Pergamon)

Premfors, Rune (1983) 'Social Research and Governmental Commissions in Sweden', *American Behavioural Scientist*, Vol 26.

Premfors, Rune (1983) *Sektorsforskningen och högskolan. En studie av en planeringsprocess*. Group for the Study of Higher Education and Research Policy, Stockholm University Report No 28.

Premfors, Rune & Wittrock, Björn (1979) 'Research and Development for Higher Education in Sweden', in *Research into Higher Education: Processes and Structures* (Stockholm: National Board of Universities and Colleges).

Thelander, Jan (1980) *Forskarutbildningen som traditionsförmedling*, 2. omarbetade upplagan, Historiska institutionen, Lunds universitet, delrapport 3.

Thelander, Jan (1982) 'Historia, teori och kunskapsutveckling. Om frågandets konst i kunskapsutvecklingen', *Scandia*, Nr 2, pp. 303–348.

Wallén, Göran (1980) *Kunskapsutveckling och organisation i tvärvetenskapliga forskningsgrupper*, Institutionen för vetenskapsteori, Göteborgs universitet (PhD dissertation, English summary)

Wallén, Göran (1982) 'The Interaction between the Development of Knowledge and Organization in the Swecon Project, Annex 2 in Sigurdsson & Granstrand, *Swedish Coniferous Forest Project Swecon* (Lund: Research Policy Institute).

Wittrock, Björn (1980) 'Långsiktig planering och forskning: inledning, *UHÄ-rapport*, 1980:14, ss 33–39.

Wittrock, Björn (1980) 'Review of Reba N Soffer, Ethics and Society in England: The Revolution in the Social Sciences 1870–1914', *Acta Sociologica*, Vol 23, No 4.

Wittrock, Björn (1980) 'Science Policy and the Challenge to the Welfare State', *West European Politics*, Vol 3, No 3.

Wittrock, Björn (1981) 'Futures Studies Without a Planning Subject: The Swedish Secretariat for Future Studies', in Baehr, P R & Wittrock, B (Eds.) *Policy Analysis and Policy Innovation* (London: Sage Publications).

Wittrock, Björn (1982) 'Managing Uncertainty or Foreclosing the Options: Futures Planning in the University of Californa', *European Journal of Education*, Vol 17, No 3.

Wittrock, Björn (1982) 'Social Knowledge, Public Policy and Social Betterment: A Review of Current Research on Knowledge Utilization in Policy-Making' *European Journal of Political Research*, Vol 10.

Wittrock, Björn (1983) 'Planning, Pluralism and Policy Intellectuals', in T Husén & M Kogan (Eds.) *Researchers and Policy-Makers in Education* (Oxford: Pergamon Press).

Wittrock, Björn (1983) 'Social Sciences Policy in Finland: Review of an OECD Report', *European Journal of Education*, Vol 18. No 2

Wittrock, Björn (1983) 'Excellence of Analysis to Diversity of Advocacy: The Multiple Roles of the Leverhulme Study into the Future of Higher Education', *Higher Education*, vol 12.

Wittrock, Björn (1983) 'Policy Analysis and Policy Making: Towards a Dispositional Model of the University/Government Interface', OECD Technical Cooperation Service Working paper (Paris: OECD)

The Educational Function

Allwood, Carl-Martin (1982) *Knowledge, techique and detection of errors in statistical problem solving*, Department of Psychology, Göteborg University (Doctoral dissertation).

Allwood, Carl-Martin (1982) 'Use of Knowledge and error detection when solving statistical problems', in Vermandel, A (Ed.) *Psychology of Mathematics Education Proceedings of the Sixth PME Conference* (Antwerpen).

Allwood, Carl-Martin & Montgomery, Henry (1981) 'Knowledge and technique in statistical problem solving', *European Journal of Science Education*, Vol 3, pp. 431–450.

Allwood, Carl-Martin & Montgomery, Henry (1982) 'Detection of errors in statistical problem solving', *Scandinavian Journal of Psychology*, Vol 23, pp. 131–139.

Dahlgren, Lars Owe (1975) *Qualitative differences in learning as a function of content-oriented guidance*, Studies in Educational Sciences, Göteborg University, No 15 (PhD disserration)

Dahlgren, Lars Owe (1979) 'Ziele und Mittel der hochschuldidaktischen Forschung und Entwicklung in Schweden und *staff development* and der Hochschule', *Zeitschrift für Hochschuldidaktik*, Vol 3, pp. 6–16.

Dahlgren, Lars Owe (1980) 'Teaching and learning in economics. – Scopes and limits', Paper presented at the congress on *Improvement of Academic Teachers' Educational Skills and Efficiency of Economic Education*, Akademia Ekonomiczna W Poznaniu, Poznan, Poland, March 25–26, 1980. (In Polish)

Dahlgren, Lars Owe & Marton, Ference (1976) 'Investigations into learning and teaching of basic concepts in economics. A research project on higher education', in Bonboir, A (Ed.) *Instructional Design in Higher Education – Innovations in Curriculum and Teaching* (Liège: Derouaux)

Dahlgren, Lars Owe & Marton, Ference (1978) 'Students' conceptions of subject matter: An aspect of learning and teaching in higher education', *Studies in Higher Education*, Vol 3, pp. 25–35.

Eriksson, Mona (1978) *Utbildningspraktik. Om utbildning med handledda klient- och patientkontakter på högskolenivå* (Practical training. On client-related training programs in higher education). Studia Psychologica et paedagogica, Lund University, No 43 (English Summar; PhD dissertation).

Falkemark, Gunnar (1982) *Power, Theory & Value*, Göteborg Studies in Politics, No 10 (Lund: CWK Gleerup) (PhD dissertation)

Franke-Wikberg, Sigbrit & Johansson, Martin (1975) *Utvärdering av undervisning. En problemanalys och några empiriska studier på universitetsnivå* (Evaluation of education. An analysis of the problems and some empirical studies in universities). Department of Education, Umeå University (English Summary; PhD dissertation)

Fransson, Anders (1976) 'Group-centred instruction – intentions and outcomes', in Entwistle, Noel J (Ed.) *Strategies for Research and Development in Higher Education* (Amsterdam: Swets & Zeitlinger).

Fransson, Anders (1977) 'On Qualitative Differences in Learning: IV. Effects of motivation and test anxiety on process and outcome', *British Journal of Educational Psychology*, Vol 47, pp. 244–257.

Halldén, Sören (1978) 'Psychomethodological terms', in Schwarz, S & Willers, U (Eds.) *Knowledge and Development – Reshaping Library and Information Services for the World of Tomorrow. A Festschrift for Björn Tell* (Stockholm: KTH's Library).

Halldén, Sören (1980) *Nyfikenhetens redskap. En bok om kritiskt tänkande inom vetenskapen och utanför* (Lund: Studentlitteratur).

Halldén, Sören (1980) 'Kunskapens nycklar', *UHÄ-rapport*, 1980:10, bd 4.

Håstad, Mats (1978) *Matematikutbildningen från grundskola till teknisk högskola, igår – idag – i morgon* (Mathematics education from primary school to higher technical education, yesterday – today – tomorrow). Department of Education, Uppsala University (English Summary; PhD dissertation).

Hesslow, Germund (1979) *Medicinsk vetenskapsteori* (Lund: Studentlitteratur).

Himmelstrand, Ulf (1974) 'Ett universitetsämnes innehåll. Utvecklingstendenser inom svensk sociologi 1967–1972', *Sociolognytt*, Nr 6.

Himmelstrand, Ulf (1977) 'Vad kan jag veta om planeringsobjektet?' *UHÄ-rapport*, 1977:20, pp. 18–31.

Himmelstrand, Ulf (1979) 'Contradiction and Innovation in Higher Education and Learning – a Research Proposal', in *Research into Higher Education: Processes and Structures* (Stockholm: National Board of Universities and Colleges), pp. 75–132.

Hjelmqvist, E, Sjöberg, L, Montgomery, H (red) (1978) *Undervisningspsykologi* (Stockholm: Almqvist & Wiksell).

Jones, Jim (1977) *Group Psychotherapy as Experiencing Interpersonal Perceiving and Developing of Values. An Integrated and Experiential Model for Practicing, Training and Researching Group Psychotherapy* (Uppsala: Almqvist & Wiksell International). (PhD dissertation)

Kallos, Daniel (1973) 'Den studerande i undervisningssituationen', i Handal, G, Holmström, L-G, Thomsen, OB (red), *Universitetsundervisning: problem, empiri, teori.* (Malmö: Studentlitteratur).

Lindahl, Lars (1975) *Effect Evaluation of Short Term Group Encounter Therapy and Evaluation of an Interpersonal Theory of Behaviour* (Uppsala: Uppsala Group Center) (PhD dissertation).

Marton, Ference (1974) 'Some Effects of Content-neutral Instructions on Non-verbatim Learning in a Natural Setting', *Scandinavian Journal of Educational Research*, Vol 18, pp. 191–210.

Marton, Ference (1975) 'On Non-verbatim Learning: I. Level of processing and level of outcome', *Scandinavian Journal of Psychology*, Vol 16, pp. 273–279.

Marton, Ference (1976) 'On Non-verbatim Learning: IV. Some theoretical and methodological notes', *Scandinavian Journal of Psychology*, Vol 17, pp. 125–128.

Marton, Ference (1976) 'On Non-verbatim Learning: II. The erosion effect of a task-induced learning algorithm', *Scandinavian Journal of Psychology*, Vol 17, pp. 41–48.

Marton, Ference (1979) 'Skill as an Aspect of Knowledge' *Journal of Higher Education*, Vol 50, No 5.

Marton, Ference & Dahlgren, Lars Owe (1976) 'On Nonverbatim Learning: III. The outcome of some basic concepts in economics', *Scandinavian Journal of Psychology*, Vol 17, pp. 49–55.

Marton, F, Dahlgren, L O, Svensson, L, Säljö, R (1977) *Inlärning och omvärldsuppfattning. En bok om den studerande människan* (Stockholm: AWE/Gebers)

Marton, Ference & Svensson, Lennart (1979) 'Conceptions of research in student learning', *Higher Education*, Vol 8, pp. 471–486.

Marton, Ference & Säljö, Roger (1976) 'On Qualitative Differences in Learning: I. Outcome and process', *British Journal of Educational Psychology*, Vol 46, pp. 4–11.

Marton, Ference & Säljö, Roger (1976) 'On Qualitative Differences in Learning: II. Outcome as a function of the learners conception of the task', *British Journal of Educational Psychology*, Vol 46, pp. 115–127.

Montgomery, Henry & Allwood, Carl-Martin (1978) 'On the subjective representation of statistical problems', *Scandinavian Journal of Educational Research*, Vol 22, pp. 107–127.

Nelsson, Olof (1976) 'Mathemagenic Activities and Teaching: A Review', *Higher Education Bulletin*, Vol 4, No 2.

Sjöberg, Lennart (1983) 'Belöning, inlärning och prestation', *Forskning om utbildning*, Nr 3, pp. 32–38.

Sjöberg, Lennart (forthcoming) 'Interest, Achievement and Vocational Choice', *European Journal of Science Education.*

Svensson, Lennart (1976) *Study Skill and Learning*, Göteborg Studies in Educational Sciences, No 19 (PhD dissertation).

Svensson, Lennart (1977) 'On Qualitative Differences in Learning: III. Study skill and learning', *British Journal of Educational Psychology*, Vol 47, pp. 233–243.

Säljö, Roger (1975) *Qualitative Differences in Learning as a Function of the Learner's Conception of the Task*, Göteborg Studies in Educational Sciences, No 14 (PhD dissertation).

Overviews, conference reports, etc

Abrahamsson, Bengt (1977) 'Om sambandet mellan forskning och grundutbildning' (The research nexus. The link between research and undergraduate teaching), *UHÄ-rapport*, 1977:10.

'Begreppsbildning och kunskapstillägnande i några universitetsämnen' (Concept formation and learning in some university subjects), *UHÄ-rapport*, 1977:3.

Bergendal, Gunnar (1983) *Knowledge and higher education* (Stockholm: Almqvist & Wiksell International).

Bergendal, G (Ed.) (forthcoming) *Knowledge Policy and Traditions in Higher Education* (Stockholm: Almqvist & Wiksell International).

Björklund, Eskil (1983) 'The Research on Higher Education Program. An Overview'. *Swedish Research on Higher Education 1983:1*. (Descriptions of the research program's content and policy, written by the head of the program's secretariat, have been published annually since 1971 in the NBUC newsletter series).

Bowman, M J, Sohlman, Åsa & Ysander, Bengt-Christer (1978) *Learning and Earning. Three Essays in the Economics of Education* (Stockholm: National Board of Universities and Colleges).

Dahlström, Edmund (1979) 'Arbetsdelning, klasskiktning och kunskapsutveckling' (Division of labour, class stratification and knowledge development), *UHÄ-rapport*, 1979:2.

Elzinga, A, Wittrock, B (Eds.) (forthcoming) *The Univesity Research System: Performance and Policy* (Stockholm: Almqvist & Wiksell International).

'Empirisk kvalifikationsforskning' (Empirical qualification research), *UHÄ-rapport*, 1981:7.

Entwistle, Noel (1976) *Strategies for research and development in higher education* (Amsterdam: Swets & Zeitlinger).

'Forskarutbildningens verksamhetsformer' (The activity forms for research training), *UHÄ-rapport*, 1973:1.

'Forskning om högskolans organisation' (Research into the organization of higher education), *UHÄ-rapport*, 1977:20.

'Forskningens villkor och möjligheter. Uppgifter för studier av forskning och forskarutbild-ning' (The conditions and potentialities of research. Tasks for studies of research and of graduate and doctoral education), *UHÄ-rapport*, 1982:9.

Grahm, Leif (red) (1980) Arbetslivsperspektiv för forskning om utbildning (Working life perspectives for research into education), *UHÄ-rapport*, 1980:9.

'Kunskapssyn och val av innehåll i några högskoleutbildningar' (Conceptions of knowledge and choices of content in some programmes of higher education), *UHÄ-rapport*, 1980:14.

'Metodproblem vid studier av relationen högre utbildning – arbetsmarknad' (Methodological problems in studies of the relation between higher education and the labour market), *UKÄ:rapport*, 1975:1.

'Metodproblem vid universitetsstudier i arbetsgrupp' (Methodological problems in university studies in groups) *UKÄ-rapport*, 1975:16.

Premfors, Rune (Ed.) (forthcoming) *Higher Education Organization. Conditions for Policy Implementation* (Stockholm: Almqvist & Wiksell International).

'Problemprecisering och initiering av forskning för området utbildning' (The specification of problems and the initiation of research for the field of education), NBUC et al, 1976.

Research into Higher Education: Processes and Structures (1979) Report from a conference (Stockholm: NBUC).

'Studier av långsiktig planering och av sektoriell forskning' (Studies of long-term planning and of sectoral research), *UHÄ-rapport*, 1980:14.

'Studier av utbildningstraditioner' (Knowledge traditions in programmes of higher education, *UHÄ-rapport*, 1980:4.

Trow, Martin (1977) 'The creation and support of a research community on higher education', *R&D for Higher Education*, 1977:3.

'Utvärdering av en högskolereform' (Evaluation of a reform of higher education), *UKÄ-rapport*, 1973:2.

Appendix 2

Selected on-going projects

Higher Education in Society

University Studies and Concept of Reality – a Study of Effects of Education

Department of Education
University of Gothenburg
P.O. Box 1010
S-431 26 MÖLNDAL
Sweden

Project leader: Ass. Prof. Lars-Owe Dahlgren

Project period: 1977–84

Abstract: The project investigates the extent and duration of the socialisation of ideas, that may be associated with different educational and disciplinary experiences in higher education. The lines of study included in the investigation are medicine, technology, psychology and economics. The method used is the longitudinal one, comprising tests, questionnaires and interviews to be administered to the students who have been selected. Interviewing will take place before, during, and at the end of their programmes of study. One question which the project hopes to answer relates to the nature of the phenomenon that is usually described as scholarly or academic thinking.

Long-Term Effects of Higher Education

Department of Education
University of Umeå
S-901 87 UMEÅ
SWEDEN

Project leader: Professor Sigbrit Franke-Wikberg

Project period: 1977–84

Abstract: The project aims to understand the different sorts of perception entertained by students about their working life, and how this is affected by different educational experiences. The researchers will follow students from four vocational backgrounds, namely medicine, engineering, psychology and economics throughout their post-secondary career. By examining the way students think and argue about their educational experiences, their future occupations and problems relating to these sectors, the researchers will endeavour to assess the differences between these four types of educational experience. The method used will be repeated in-depth interviewing, over a long period, with a selected sample of students.

Long-Term Effects of Education Among Post-Secondary Students

Department of Education
University of Gothenburg
Box 1010
S-431 26 MÖLNDAL
SWEDEN

Project leader: Professor Kjell Härnqvist

Project period: 1979–84

Abstract: This project forms part of a wider programme being jointly pursued in the Department of Educational Research at the University of Gothenburg, and it makes use of a growing body of empirical data associated with that programme. Its aim is to study the educational background of selected undergraduate students and its consequences for their subsequent careers. The methods of the inquiry are postal questionnaire and survey followed by in-depth interviews with selected respondents.

Working Life, Education and Planning

Department of Political Science
University of Stockholm
and
Department of Educational Research
Stockholm Institute of Education
P O Box 34103
S-100 26 STOCKHOLM
SWEDEN

Project leader: Dr. Bo Lindensjö

Project period: 1981–84

Abstract: This project examines public policy which links higher education with working life, with attention to both the implementation as well as the formulation stages of policy development. Plans made by authorities and planning agencies in this domain will be analysed to see whether they present a uniform policy, whether they are mutually consistant. The study of implementation will be comparative and deal with different types of higher education – traditional, academic studies and new higher education programmes.

Technical Knowledge and Vocational Identity

Department of Sociology
University of Lund
Box 5132
S-220 05 LUND
SWEDEN

Project leader: Dr Boel Berner

Project period: 1982–86

Abstract: The project investigates the content and transmission of technical knowledge in upper-sec, which students assimilate and/or modify according to their own backgrounds and social attitudes. The project will analyse the qualification process with the aid of three concepts: technical competence, technical/professional values, and technical culture, which relate respectively to cognitive learning, discipline, and world views imparted by technical education. The investigation will be based on studies and intensive interviews of two upper-secondary school and two technical faculties, and on the analysis of statistical material, essays, curricula, historical and other documentary material, plus questionnaire surveys.

Knowledge, Attitudes and Values in Computer Programming

Department of Technology and Social Change
University of Linköping
S-581 83 LINKÖPING
SWEDEN

Project leaders: Professor Lars Ingelstam and
Anders Beckman, research assistent

Project period: 1983–86

Abstract: Knowledge production processes, at all levels, will be faced with far-reaching demands for understanding and competences posed by computerisation. These demands have long-term implications for higher education.

The purpose of the project is to increase our understanding of the interaction of technology, knowledge, attitudes and values in the programming of computers. It will investigate such characteristics of information technologies as formalisation, predetermination and restrictions of flexibility, how different types of knowledge about programming are developed and transmitted and how programming work is influenced by knowledge, attitudes and values.

The project involves a number of case studies about the work of programmers and a study of the development of programming as a profession, together with a study of attitudes and values as they relate to working with information technology.

Higher Education as an Organisation

Ideology, Science and Society

Department of History of Ideas
University of Gothenburg
Västra Hamngatan 3
S-411 17 GÖTEBORG
SWEDEN

Project leaders: Professor Sven-Eric Liedman and
Ass. Prof. Ingemar Nilsson

Project period: 1979–82

Abstract: The project studies from an interdisciplinary perspective the origins and development of the medical profession in four countries, Sweden, Denmark, Britain and
France. It draws on a variety of modes of enquiry, historical, sociological and
comparative with a view to understanding the nature of the hierarchy and
professionalisation to be found among practitioners of medicine.

Ideologies of Education and Research in the Health Care Sector

Department of Theory of Science
University of Gothenborg
Västra Hamngatan 3
S-411 17 GÖTEBORG
SWEDEN

Project team: Ass. Prof. Aant Elzinga,
Ass. Prof. Jan Bärmark and
Ass. Prof. Göran Wallén

Project period: 1979–83

Abstract: The project's aim is to investigate some of the areas of knowledge which have been
recently incorporated into the Swedish system of Higher Education, and which
traditionally were not included within definitions of academic study. The main
discipline to be investigated is nursing, and the teaching of nursing care, and to a
lesser extent physical therapy and radiology. The method is to interview persons who
have followed, or who intend to follow Ph. D. programmes in these areas, as well as
those who are responsible for the supervision or direction of these programmes of
study.

The Emergence and Development of Training for Social Workers in Sweden

Department of Sociology
University of Göteborg
Karl Johansgatan 27
S-414 59 Göteborg, SWEDEN

Project leaders: Professor Edmund Dahlström and
Esbjörn Johansson, BA

Project period: 1979–81

Abstract: This project entails an analysis of the training of social workers in Sweden, from the first modest beginnings with the courses arranged in the 1910s by the Central Union for Social Work (CSA) down to the Social Study Program of the present-day higher education system. It ties in with concept and theory formation in sociology of science and sociology of knowledge and with the sociology of education which has been developed at the Department of Sociology at the University of Gothenburg. At the same time this work is intended to contribute to a certain development of concepts and models. – The project has been delayed and will be reported in 1984.

Knowledge Traditions in the Education of Pre-School Teachers

Department of Education
University of Göteborg
Box 1010
S-431 26 MÖLNDAL
SWEDEN

Project leaders: Professor Ference Marton and
Jan-Erik Johansson, M.A.

Project period: 1981–84

Abstract: This project describes and analyses 'pre-school methods' in Swedish pre-school teacher education and how this subject has been perceived by teachers of pre-school methods. Pre-school teacher-training programmes are examples of non- academic education which was incorporated into the Swedish higher education system in the reforms of 1977.
The initial premise is that considerable variability exists between 'pre-school' methods and 'infant education', and that this variation is related to changes that have occured both in the pre-schools themselves, and in the education of pre-school teachers.
The study is based on interviewing teachers of pre-school methods, on discussions of the preliminary analysis with groups of teachers of this subject area, and on the analysis of written documents.
The methodological approach adopted draws upon a research tradition that studies people's perceptions of their surroundings (i.e. how they structure their reality), on historical studies of knowledge development, and on sociological studies of the development of higher education professions. Written materials will be collected to contrast developments in the 1930's and 1940's with those in the 1970's.

Bureaucrats, Education, and the Administration of Society

Department of History
Uppsala University
S:t Larsgatan 2
S752 20 UPPSALA
SWEDEN

Project leaders: Professor Rolf Torstendahl and
Dr. Svenbjörn Kilander

Project period: 1982-85

Abstract: The purpose of the project is to analyse the education of Swedish bureaucrats and administrators with respect to the ideological content of that education. Does the view of State and society change over time? The problem is being studied in the context of the development of industrial society between 1890 and 1935, with particular reference to the post-secondary education of engineers, economists, lawyers and social scientists. Source materials will include text books, compendia and the reports of official enquiries.

Institution and Ideology 1880–1980

Department of History of Ideas
University of Gothenburg
Västra Hamngatan 3
S-411 17 GÖTEBORG
SWEDEN

Project leaders: Professor Sven-Eric Liedman and
Dr. Lennart Olausson

Project period: 1983–86

Abstract: An investigation of the connection between the outward organisation of the university, its relation to public administration, its position in society, and certain central complexes of ideas developing and flourishing within the university. The study focuses on Sweden, but comparisons with other countries are of central importance. Its concern will be with three periods: 1890–1900, the 1930's and, finally the 1960's and 1970's.

Liberty, Responsibility and Science.
Student Organizations 1945–1965

Department of History of Ideas
University of Stockholm
S-106 91 STOCKHOLM
SWEDEN

Project leader: Professor Nils Runeby

Project period: 1983–85

Abstract: This project concerns itself with the compilation of an inventory of materials with a view to planning a study in the history of ideas devoted to student organizations and associations between 1945 and 1965. It follows an earlier study about Liberal and Social Democratic associations; the ideas of intellectuals and students concerning science and society will be discussed in this context.

The Research Function

Practitioners and Social Scientists. Planning and the Utilization of Social Science

Department of Sociology
University of Göteborg
Karl Johansgatan 27
S-414 59 GÖTEBORG
SWEDEN

Project leaders: Professor Edmund Dahlström and
                        Esbjörn Johansson, BA

Project period: 1977–80

Abstract: This project contains analyses of the relations between practitioners and researchers in three fields: consumer policy, working life policy and higher education policy. The project has been delayed and will be reported in 1984.

The Culture and Community of Research

Department of Sociology
University of Lund
Box 5132
S-220 05 LUND
SWEDEN

Project leader: Dr. Katrin Fridjonsdottir

Project period: 1982–86

Abstract: This project investigates the interplay of cognitive, social and institutional factors in university-based scientific research.
    The project will be carried out in the following three phases:
    1 Historical and theoretical studies in order to prepare for the empirical work.
    2 Data collection at Swedish universities. Two generations of scientific researchers will be studied.
    3 Data analysis.

The Use of Sectoral Research

Group for the Study of Higher Education
and Research Policy
Department of Political Science
University of Stockholm
S-106 91 STOCKHOLM
SWEDEN

Project leader: Ass. Prof. Rune Premfors

Project period: 1982–85

Abstract: There are in Sweden some 50 or 60 agencies devoted to the task of research and development which are the manifestation of the government's policy of sectoral research. The project aims to subject this policy to analytic scrutiny. The problems to be investigated include the following. What are the positions and resources of the sectoral R & D agencies within their sectors? How are the R & D agencies governed? Which types of knowledge are they trying to develop? To what extent and with what methods are R & D results utilised and disseminated?

A series of seminars is planned which will scrutinise selected R & D agencies.

The Educational Function

Study Skill in Mechanics

Department of Education
University of Göteborg
P O Box 1010
S-431 26 MÖLNDAL
SWEDEN

Project leader: Associate Professor Lennart Svensson

Project period: 1978–83

Abstract: The purpose of the project is to study technology students' understanding and learning in mechanics. The study proceeds from the concept of "study skill" developed previously with the purpose of developing further and extending the previous descriptions to a natural science/technology content. We see ourselves arriving at descriptions of decisive differences in understanding of physical phenomena and descriptions of what is characteristic of study activities which lead to differing understanding. Here we chiefly make use of physical phenomena for an explanation of which the force concept of classical mechanics is of direct relevance. The aspect of study skill we concentrate chiefly on is the cognitive approach or direction in thinking.

Intellectual Maturity as an Educational Ideal

Department of Philosophy
University of Lund
Kungshuset, Lundagård
S-223 50 LUND
SWEDEN

Project leader: Professor Sören Halldén

Project period: 1981–86

Abstract: The project concerns itself with the student's self-directedness, determined by his/her attitude to life, feeling for quality and essentiality, and with his/her opinions concerning techniques of knowledge acquisition. A descriptive study will be made of the occurence of different types of ideas about self-direction and similar notions. The main emphasis will be on the analysis of written material.

Study Interest

Department of Psychology
University of Göteborg
Box 14158
S-400 20 GÖTEBORG
SWEDEN

Project leader: Professor Lennart Sjöberg

Project period: 1979–84

Abstract: This project develops methods for measuring factors of interest in mathematics, science and technology. These methods relate to preferences for technical and scientific occupations among students in terminal classes of the technical and scientific lines of upper secondary schools.

A study will also be made of freshmen (sophomores) at technical faculties. Special attention being paid to the connection between interest and educational achievement/drop-out. It also intends to investigate the factors of interest in certain social scientific and humanist studies so as to contrast them with the interest factors we have formulated for science and technology.

Subject-Didactic Studies of Research Training in Biology and Physics

Department of Education
University of Gothenburg
Box 1010
S-431 26 MÖLNDAL
SWEDEN

Project leader: Ass. Professor Leif Lybeck

Project period: 1983–86

Abstract: The project will study the phenomenon of research training in a content-oriented pedagogical perspective. Its purpose are as follows:

1 To chart the content of concepts entertained by tutors and post-graduate students of research training, by means of interview studies, and to relate these concepts to their conceptions of subject-range, knowledge, science and research.

2 To chart aspects of the content of research training and the relationship between tutor and post-graduate student.

3 To study the outward conditions applying to research training within the disciplines selected.

The theoretical framework comprises the pedagogical research approach developed at the Department of Education, University of Gothenburg by the INOM Group – the phenomenographical approach. The qualitative view of pedagogical knowledge development, is expressed in the interview method and in the process of analysis which lead to descriptions of certain phenomena or concepts. These approaches to the study of pedagogical processes supplement those dealing with organisational and economic aspects. The results are expected to be conducive to improvements in the content and design of research training, particularly as regards tutoring.

Education for the Application of Statistics.
A Study of Knowledge Perspectives

Department of Philosophy
University of Uppsala
Box 256
S-751 05 UPPSALA
SWEDEN

Project leader: Dr. Bengt Molander

Project period: 1983–87

Abstract: The purpose of this project is to examine in a historical and comparative perspective the capacity acquired by students for applying statistics critically and with reflection (both within pure statistics and in its broader application). It will also examine the conceptions of cognition of students, teachers and practicing statisticians of *various* kinds together with their views concerning the role of statistics.

The study will employ content analysis of programme and goal documents, analysis of teaching materials (in various subjects and traditions) and, finally, interviews and participant observation.